▼

Also by Barbara Ensrud

THE POCKET GUIDE TO WINE

THE POCKET GUIDE TO CHEESE

AMERICAN VINEYARDS

▼

A FIRESIDE BOOK

PUBLISHED BY SIMON & SCHUSTER

NEW YORK · LONDON · TORONTO

SYDNEY · TOKYO · SINGAPORE

Wine

WITH ▾ FOOD

a guide to entertaining
through the seasons

BARBARA ENSRUD

Foreword by M. F. K. Fisher

FIRESIDE

Simon & Schuster Building
Rockefeller Center
1230 Avenue of the Americas
New York, New York, 10020

Designed by Liney Li
Manufactured in the United States of America

10 9 8 7 6 5 4 3 2 1 Pbk.

Library of Congress Cataloging in Publication Data

Ensrud, Barbara.
Wine with food : a guide to entertaining through the seasons /
Barbara Ensrud ; foreword by M.F.K. Fisher ; illustrations by
Beatriz Vidal.
p.   cm.
"A Fireside book."
Originally published: New York : Congdon & Weed, © 1984.
Includes index.
1. Wine and wine making.   2. Entertaining.   3. Menus.   I. Title.
[TP548.E57   1991]
642'.4—dc20   91–26793
                                          CIP

ISBN: 0-671-68714-X Pbk.

CONTENTS

ACKNOWLEDGMENTS

My years of involvement with wine have brought me in contact with many wonderful people who understood the art of eating and drinking well. Directly or indirectly, they have helped shape my sensibilities, and I am eternally grateful to all of them.

Specifically for this volume, I wish to express special thanks to my editor Sydny Miner of Fireside Books, and to Lea Guyer Gordon, who first proposed doing the book; and to Mary Frances Fisher, whose gentle encouragement has been so supportive.

My deep appreciation goes also to Sam and Florence Aaron, Franklin Avery, Peter and Nanno Bienstock, Darrell Corti, Narsai David, Faith Echtemeyer, Julia Child, Mireille Giuliano, Stan Goldberg, Lila Jaeger, Ted Kaplan, Paul Kovi, Tom Margittai, Louis P. Martini, Anita Mizener, Rebecca Murphy, Helen Niemi, Léonce Picot, Bernard and Belle Rhodes, Henry Rubin, Rosita Sarnoff, Shirley Sarvis, Arthur Schwartz, Janet Trefethen, Penelope Wisner, and Dr. Jurg Zutt.

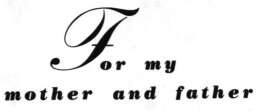

For my
mother and father

FOREWORD

Simple: Opposite of complex; straightforward.
(Definition of word used in wine-judging,
Wine with Food, page 219)

This is, in more than one way, a good description of the book. It is also a good one of Barbara Ensrud's style, and of her subtle yet very uncomplicated approach to the whole overly fussy subject of marrying wines to dishes, and good drinking to good eating.

Books about gastronomy run in seasonal patterns, and presently many of them are written as if winter, spring, summer, and autumn had been invented within the past two or three years for the sole purpose of making life simpler for writers about the pleasures of the table. Before this we have seen alphabets and calendars and even decades and centuries used mercilessly by many fine to dreadful scriveners, in their efforts to justify "one more book" on the general topic of hunger itself. Inevitably most of them will be forgotten, and rightly so.

Now and then, though, an attempt to explain our natural preoccupation with keeping ourselves alive and well and relatively happy seems meant to be read for a long time, and I think this book is one of them. I hope so, for good things should not be let disappear, and I feel that *Wine with Food* is written with skill and real honesty about something often murked over, today, by prejudices and affectations and plain snobbery.

But here and now, at least in Barbara Ensrud's book, the air is clear and sunny (or perhaps in winter properly cold, with a good hungry snap to it), and we can be as trusting as innocent children that what we eat will match to perfection what we are given to drink. (Of course, milk and hot cocoa go by the boards in this mature counseling, but once Bloody Marys are advised with complete rightness, to start a picnic or perhaps a tailgate booster, or where any wine would be impossible with the suggested food. . . .)

Barbara's sureness about this pairing is almost uncanny, at least to my own mental palate. Perhaps it is because I agree with her, most of the time! Perhaps I like this book about what I would choose to drink with what I am eating because I wish I had said it myself!

For instance, I like what she writes about rosé wines. She "keeps hoping" that here in our wine-rich country they will be made drier and more simply, less pompously. We take rosés too seriously, she and I agree. It is as if the vintners are trying to pretend that rosés are indeed *not* "picnic wines" and certainly *not* vintage, but still not the good go-down easy drinkin' stuff that they should be. And it warms my weary heart to hear such a firm clear voice as Barbara's speaking out. We both know rosés well, and how they can be plain and still subtle, and sturdier than dry whites but never pretentious.

There are many other reasons for my liking this book and the personal but detached way the author has written it.

It is evocative, as all good reading should be. Once she says something about what to serve with the ceremonial turkey that is part of our traditional Thanksgiving, and I think at once of how my mother always insisted on serving a pale dry sherry with that hallowed bird, instead of the Johannisberg or bubbly that my father really preferred.

In other words, this book is not only helpful and reassuring, but it makes us think far past and beyond it, and I like that. Barbara Ensrud tells us that what we have already known will help us say yes or no to many of our future temptations and enjoyments, and that "given the chance," we can know even more! *Good!*

M. F. K. Fisher
Glen Ellen, California

INTRODUCTION

Wine and food as natural companions have long been taken for granted in gastronomical circles, but only recently in this country has the enjoyment of wine become something for everyone. A plethora of cookbooks takes care of our endless curiosity for new ways with food. I am happy to note that many more of them include wine suggestions.

In the first edition of *Wine with Food*, I lamented the lack of guidance for pairing the two. Since then, little more than half a decade later, there are a couple of good books on the subject, as well as newsletters, pamphlets, classes, and a greater focus in magazines and other media. As I noted back then, there is a genuine eagerness to make the best possible choice to go with specific foods. "I have a haunch of venison I've been saving for a special occasion," one man said to me after a wine class. "What is the really ultimate match for it?" I gave him a few suggestions for what *might* result in the "ultimate match," if there is such a thing. There are simply no guarantees. Just as beauty lies in the eye of the beholder, the exquisite mating of wine with food rests, ultimately, on the palate of the taster.

This book, then, is a wine lover's approach to gastronomy. It reflects a rather personal philosophy, as you will see, but it should serve more as a starting point or stimulus than as any sort of rigid mandate. The guidelines are mostly general, but sometimes quite specific. I have not hesitated to express personal preferences, specific wines, and certain combinations that I have come to like. I am well aware that opinions will differ from mine in some instances, just as they do at the dinner table, but to me that is all part of the fun. One can get into spirited discussions of what goes with what. As long as the exchange is convivial and open-minded, I delight in it and welcome it.

If the book seems more concerned with meals for entertaining than with day-to-day fare, it is because the need seems greatest there. Even so, you will find that many of the wines suggested are moderately priced and eminently suited for casual occasions, from picnics to weekend brunches.

The seasonal approach I have taken may seem a bit arbitrary, but the tremendous emphasis today on seasonal foods and dishes is largely what prompted it. Certainly there are wines we drink year-round without regard to season. There are also wines with a close affinity to certain times of year or to certain dishes prepared with strong seasonal emphasis. Thus a given wine may be discussed in spring as well as fall, but the context in each case will be quite different. As a device, the seasonal emphasis served as a useful focus for me, but it should not in any way be looked upon as constraining. On the contrary, the intent here is to encourage people to be as freewheeling as they like. By all means, accept the urge to experiment, make substitutions, invent combinations of your own. This book should serve as a jumping-off point. The possibilities are limitless. It would be impossible to give them all in a single book.

I must also point out that this book is not intended as a guide to wines of the world. There are many excellent primers and weightier tomes that give history and background on the wines commonly encountered by most of us, and it would be good to have one at your elbow for reference. A good general introduction to the subject can be found in *The New Signet Book of Wine* by Alexis Bespaloff, and more specific information in Hugh Johnson's *Modern Encyclopedia* and the encyclopedias of Alexis Lichine and Frank Schoonmaker (revised by Mr. Bespaloff). The pocket guides, those that cover wines of the world or specific regions such as Italy or California, can also be useful for quick reference.

A Note on the Menus

The menu suggestions are drawn from those in my own repertoire. I am a reasonably good cook and occasionally even invent my own recipes. But mostly, as more of a wine specialist than a food specialist, I rely on the recipes of experts I admire. In the back of this book is a bibliography of the cookbooks to which I frequently refer and which contain versions of the dishes recommended in the menus.

WITH ▾ FOOD

Chapter 1

CHANGING
STYLES,
CHANGING
RULES

▼

*Americans are just beginning to regard food the way the
French always have. Dinner is not what you do in the
evening before something else. Dinner is the evening.*

ART BUCHWALD

*I*n the years since this book was first written, American gastronomy has put forth shoots that reach into every region of the country, fostering an American cuisine as varied in influence and expression as our melting pot heritage could make it. The decade of the eighties, whatever else it is remembered for, will stand forever as the seminal decade in our country's gastronomic history. Regional foods and ways of cooking, a bevy of talented chefs, regional wines, and a veritable explosion of farmstead cheeses have emerged to create a uniquely American contribution to world gastronomy. It is still evolving, and will continue to—amid the rise and fall of fads we Americans are so prone to, and despite the excesses of some practitioners who go overboard to create something "original." American cuisine is still a work in progress, an ever-expanding crazy quilt of rich diversity and flavor.

The way we dine has evolved as much as the food we eat. A century ago dinner at eight was a formal affair here as it was in Europe, an evening marathon that involved anywhere from eight to fourteen courses, with at least as many wines. Such a feast took hours, with one or two breaks for entremets, small dishes of sorbet or sherbet designed to refresh the palate (and the brain, no doubt!), shrink the contents of the stomach, and make room for more.

These dinners were mainstays at a certain level of society, the atmosphere typically loaded with political or romantic intrigue, often both. Scintillating descriptions of such dinners exist; yet many of them must have been incredibly boring, tedious enough to prompt one powerful society matron around the turn of the century to institute what became known as the fifty-minute dinner—three courses that could be served and consumed in under an hour. This left the remainder of the evening free for the theater or the opera, but gave short shrift to the pleasures of the table. Prohibition further encouraged this truncated repast (appetizer, main course, dessert) by outlawing a vital constituent: wine, along with all other alcoholic beverages save those "medicinal" or sacramental. As a result, the art of dining in this country was almost obliterated.

It took years for Americans to get back into the swing of spending an entire evening enjoying dinner—as Art Buchwald, one of our national wits who also happens to be a gourmand of note, has cannily observed. Increasing infatuation with good food, and the wines that go with it, has reestablished the dinner party as evening entertainment in and of itself. Once again, there is time to linger and to savor, to exchange views. Once again, the art of conversation flourishes, as the wheels of social intercourse are oiled and sweetened by the flow of good food and drink. Or so we like to think.

This scene occurs at many levels today, from simple suburban households to urban apartments to the East Wing of the White House, and just as in Thomas Jefferson's day or among our Victorian forebears, intriguing things transpire at table. New alliances are forged, or broken; affairs of state may take a subtle turn; flirtations sally back and forth across the table, arousing hopes, or jealousies, or who knows what passion. "Since Eve ate apples," wrote Byron in *Don Juan*, "much depends on dinner."

However luscious the food or grand the wine, they can do little for each other unless they are well matched. Yet when they are, when the two conform and interact, twine about each other in sinuous harmony, mutually attuned to every subtle nuance or bright intensity of flavor, it is a partnership sublime, like two lovers, each bringing the other to new heights of pleasure and perception.

Such a union rarely comes about automatically; it takes some thought and is based on experience, which is why any and every meal provides useful opportunity for discovery. Restaurants where the owner takes special interest in wine are often a wonderful source for discovering brilliant combinations. One in particular that I recall was a dinner at the DownUnder, a wine restaurant in Fort Lauderdale, Florida. I pondered the menu, trying to decide which among dozens of dishes listed would best accompany a special Chardonnay. The wine was a 1975 Mayacamas, which I knew to be fairly okay. In the mid-1970s, most California Chardonnays were liberally laced with the flavor of oak, greatly overdone in some cases, although this one was not. The Mayacamas Chardonnay was about eight years old at the time, so I knew the oakiness would be fairly prominent in the wine.

All this was more or less at the back of my mind, for we were having several of owner Léonce Picot's cellar treasures that evening and we were being very careful about what we ordered. Then one dish caught my eye: lobster on a bed of spinach in a cream sauce flavored with vanilla bean. That was it, of course. Vanillin is a component of oak, and Chardonnays aged in oak are often described as having vanilla flavors. Vanilla extracted from the bean and vanillin extracted from oak are not exactly the same, but the flavors are very similar in how we perceive them. It turned out to be one of the most stunning combinations I have ever experienced. The wine sauce with the lobster had just the right accent of vanilla; with air the wine blossomed, unfurling a rich mingle of spicy fruit and wood.

That, to be sure, is the marriage of food and wine at its best. But like marriage, one cannot always be certain that the combination will prove so blissful. One brings what one knows to the affiliation and sometimes the union is exciting, sometimes banal; sometimes it simply does not work at all and the contenders fight to a standoff. That same evening, in fact, the wine that worked so well with the lobster was completely wrong with a trio of elaborately cooked oysters—Rockefeller, Muscovite, and Savannah—so pungently flavored they would have wrought havoc with almost any white wine. A dry white Graves or Pinot Gris would have been a better choice in that case.

We are not to concern ourselves here, however, with only the loftiest combinations. Food and wine match-ups at more plebeian levels, such as sausages and Beaujolais, can bring just as much satisfaction, and happily, the sense of elation they induce is likely to be more frolicsome than sublime.

The rules for what goes with what have loosened up considerably in recent decades. The day is gone when a lineup of foods and wines must follow some Procrustean format of arbitrary rules. Looking at certain modern match-ups, in fact—white wine with everything, Bordeaux with oysters—one might conclude that the old maxims of white with fish and red with meat had been tossed to the wind. They have not; they still work supremely well in many cases. While we are freer today to match up things purely in terms of personal preference, it would be a shame to miss something sensational by ignoring the traditional rules altogether. Bordeaux with lamb, Sauternes with foie gras, oysters with Chablis—these are classics that can mate equally well with other partners, but not necessarily better. It would be well to experience certain time-honored pairings at least once and let your palate be the judge.

The freedom to mix and match is a sign, I believe, of how much more relaxed we are about serving wine, which is all to the good. Wine has lost some of the mystique that made it forbidden territory for a lot of people. It has gradually eased itself into our way of life as a beverage of moderation and conviviality, a role it has played in human society since the earliest days of civilization. "And Noah began to be a husbandman, and he planted a vineyard. . . ."

Selecting wine involves more than just a casual consideration of the food; the style of the dish and the ingredients used in it have a great deal to say about the choice. The dish and the wine should complement one another, not compete. Highly seasoned dishes need wines that can hold their own against assertive flavors, where wines of subtlety or intricate complexity would be overwhelmed. With certain Chinese dishes, for example, people (if they prefer wine to beer) often choose dry Gewürztraminer, whose forthright spiciness is not cowed by the likes of ginger chicken or Hunan spiced shrimp. With Thanksgiving turkey and its spicy trimmings one of the best choices is California Zinfandel, whose garrulous fruit stands up handily to the riot of flavors on the table all at once—candied sweet potatoes, mashed turnips, stuffing with herbs, sausage, or oysters, cranberry sauce, and other condiments.

A simple grilled fish such as sole or trout, by contrast, needs a delicate wine, although certainly it can be one with subtle nuance and complexity, like a *Kabinett* Riesling from Germany, or one of the white Burgundies from the Mâcon region, such as Saint-Véran. More flavorful fish, such as striped bass, red snapper, or turbot, calls for a bigger wine, especially if it is served with an herb-flavored *beurre blanc*. Here one turns to the full-bodied whites, California Chardonnay or Burgundies like Meursault or Puligny-Montrachet, with their wonderful oak-scented perfume and silken texture. With meatier fish like salmon, tuna, or swordfish, red wines such as Pinot Noir or a red Burgundy, even a supple Merlot, are preferable to white wine.

One of the best examples of a food that defies generalizing as far as wines go is pasta. Pasta dishes come in countless variations. Many different wines, both red and white, are suitable with pasta, depending on the sauce and flavorings. Meat sauces require a sturdy red like Barbera d'Alba or Montepulciano d'Abruzzo, cream sauces are better with a dry white like Gavi or Trentino Chardonnay, simple butter and garlic go well with a chilled Grignolino or Chiaretto del Garda. (See pasta chart, pages 103–105.)

Well-matured red wines like Bordeaux, Cabernet Sauvignons from California, Italian Barbarescos, Gattinara, and other medium-bodied reds are best served with foods that allow the complex flavors and aromas they develop with age to fully reveal themselves. Roast meats are a frequent choice for such wines. Roast leg of lamb, for instance, creates a splendid backdrop for a fine Cabernet or Bordeaux. The rich and herblike flavors of Cabernet Sauvignon (the grape predominant in many of the best Bordeaux) merge superbly with the distinctive flavor of the meat and the herbs commonly used to season it, such as rosemary.

More robust dishes, meats enveloped in wine-dark sauces, savory meat stews, and the like, need more vigorous wines—the big Rhônes, Barolo or Brunello di Montalcino, Petite Sirah. These wines can also handle the stronger cheeses, such as Dry Jack, aged Gouda, Parmigiano-Reggiano, Pont l'Evêque, or sharp Cheddar— but so can fruit-packed reds like Dolcetto d'Alba and California Rhône blends such as Le Cigare Volant or Cotes Sauvages.

We are not talking here only about the flavor and intensity of various wines, but also about body and texture, the way the wine feels in the mouth. Some wines are rich and chewy; these are often young reds that still have a lot of tannin, that astringent, puckery character that can be quite harsh. Meat, cheese, or any food rich in protein or fat has a mellowing effect on tannin. The most obvious example is that of adding milk to tea, which contains a lot of tannin. Thus, a young, tannic red will be more enjoyable to drink with a robust meat dish, with cheese, or with a dish that incorporates cheese.

Acidity and sweetness are critical considerations, too. Acidity gives wine its liveliness and vitality. Wines that lack sufficient acidity taste dull and flabby; they sort of die on the palate. Good acidity is crucial for a wine to age, particularly white wines. One reason the better French whites from Burgundy and Bordeaux can last five, six, or even ten years is the high level of acidity that gives the wine the structure to age. The actual acidity in French wines is not always higher in measurement than the California wines, but it is proportionately higher in relation to other elements (tannin, fruit sugars, alcohol), all of which tend to be lower. Acidity must, however, be in balance with the fruit. Wines made from grapes that did not ripen enough will often be overly acidic, sharp, and unpleasant. Sweet wines, however, need particularly high acidity to keep them from being insipid or cloying. Interestingly, the naturally sweet wines like Sauternes or late-harvest Rieslings have an unusually high degree of acid, due to the work of a mold (*Botrytis cinerea*, often referred to as "noble rot") that transforms them into honeyed nectar. In wines of more moderate sweetness, including many of the Rieslings, Chenin Blancs, and Gewürztraminers of California, high acidity makes them seem less sweet. The cooler climates of Oregon and New York both yield wines much higher in acidity than is common in the sunnier regions of California. Chilling, incidentally, will blunt the sweetness to some extent— a good thing to remember for inexpensive wines that are sweeter than you would like them to be.

Foods That Fight Wines

Certain foods ruin the flavor of wine, others merely nullify it. Vinegar and condiments that contain it, like mustards, pickles, salad dressings, relishes, and such, are antagonistic to wine. The powerful acidity of vinegar makes wine taste flat, which is why wine and salad are not served together. The influence of nouvelle cuisine, however, has encouraged the use of rarefied fruit and herb vinegars in sauces and pasta dishes. If used judiciously they can add an appealing note of piquancy but are more compatible with wines that are higher in acidity, like those made from Sauvignon Blanc (Sancerre, Fumé Blanc), Orvieto, or Italian reds like Barolo, Nebbiolo, or Chianti.

Very spicy foods, particularly those that contain hot spices like chilies or peppercorns, can overwhelm all but the staunchest wines. Beer is often a better choice with such foods, or simple refreshing wine drinks that can be served very cold, like sangria with Mexican food. Salty foods can prove difficult with most wines, although the brisk froth of Champagne or sparkling wines cuts through the intensity very well. That is why Champagne makes such a good aperitif with savory canapés or with caviar.

Some wage arguments for only vodka with caviar—I like it, too, iced and neat with Beluga or Osetra. This is a potent combination, however, and may be too much to precede a multicourse dinner with several wines. In this context, Champagne is probably a wiser choice. Sparkling wines can also handle smoked foods quite well, as can dry fortified wines like fino Sherry or manzanilla.

Other foods that kill the taste of any wine are anchovies, citrus (grapefruit more than lemon), mayonnaise, chocolate, and sweets that are intensely syrupy or sugary. Lemon, a prime citrus fruit, is a questionable inclusion here. Like vinegar, it is frequently used as an accent to liven up many different foods, fish certainly, but also the blander meats like veal or pork. Use lemon with a light and gentle hand and you can serve almost any wine with it. Some people feel that heavy reds can handle chocolate, but having tried some of these combinations—dark, tannic Cabernets, for instance, and old Barolo, which is occasionally served in northern Italy with chocolate—I have yet to find a pairing that works as well for the wine as it does the chocolate. The best wine with chocolate is black Muscat. The berryish flavors marry nicely with chocolate, as in chocolate cake with raspberry layers.

There are some foods that do not really fight wine, but they can be difficult to mate. Eggs, for example, are rarely enhanced by any wine, although a light or medium-bodied red is often the best choice for omelets. Fruity whites like Chenin Blanc or dry French Colombard are also sometimes recommended, though I have never found them very successful. It's the sulphur in eggs that makes them difficult for wine. Some experts say that no wine goes with artichokes or asparagus; I disagree.

These foods are quite commonly served as a first course, and are often an emphatic presence with the main course. One of the delights of traveling in Europe in May is the preponderance of white asparagus, plumper but more delicate than the green asparagus prevalent here. The European variety would be green like American asparagus, but growing techniques are different. When the stalks reach the early stages of ripening, dirt is piled high around them to shield them from the sun. Maturing in the dark, they remain white and very tender.

The Europeans do not forgo wine with asparagus. On the contrary, villages that grow especially fine asparagus make a festival of the season. And what would a festival be without wine? One May, traveling from Frankfurt to Baden-Baden, I got off the train in Mannheim to have lunch with a friend from Heidelberg. On a previous visit I had raved about the wonderful asparagus I had had in France. "The next time you visit," he told me, "if the time is right, I will take you to a restaurant in Schwetzingen that serves nothing but asparagus for a month."

So here I was, and the time was right. The annual asparagus festival in Schwetzingen was in full swing, and we took off for Biba's favorite restaurant. We began with a light fish appetizer, and then came the main course: a heaping platter of asparagus, dozens of steaming white stalks with purple tips. The waiter brought ramekins of lemon butter and a sauceboat of hollandaise, and we gorged to our hearts' content. We drank a fresh local Sylvaner with the asparagus. It was just right—fruity, light-bodied, off-dry.

In France, dry white wines from the Loire Valley or Mâcon Blanc usually accompany asparagus. I discovered in Germany, however, that a light touch of sweetness in wines like Sylvaner (or Riesling, or Gewürztraminer) can suit asparagus very nicely. California wines such as Chenin Blanc, particularly such Chenin as Preston or Hacienda, would also be appropriate. If asparagus is served with lemon, a light vinaigrette, or hollandaise sauce, Fumé Blanc or Sauvignon Blanc might be a better choice; its crisp acidity can stand up to tartness and also makes it a better mate for the rich sauce. Consider as well one of the pleasantly tart Italian Sauvignons from the northeastern regions of Friuli or Tre Venezie.

For similar reasons, Sauvignon Blanc suits artichokes with lemon butter. Artichoke vinaigrette, however, may be too strong for any wine, though young, fresh Orvieto is a possibility.

Two important trends are fostering the need for new considerations of wine with food: the proliferation of ethnic cuisines and the emergence of regional American foods and cooking styles. What to drink with mesquite-grilled swordfish? I recommend a red Burgundy along the lines of Santenay or Pommard, an Oregon Pinot Noir, or a light Merlot. If you prefer white, however, try an oak-aged Sauvignon Blanc such as Carmenet or Vichon Chevrignon. With Thai beef salad? If not beer, than Alsace Riesling or Soave. How about crawfish étouffée? I would choose a light red such as Pinot Noir or Mercurey, or perhaps a chillable red like Beaujolais or Gamay. With couscous? A *vin gris* or dry rosé, as is the custom in Morocco and Tunisia. There are many new avenues to explore. I've also included sections for several popular food categories: Oriental (pages 143–46), Mediterranean (pages 147–48), Mexican and the Southwest (page 149). Chapter Seven (page 139) as well as "Wine and Food: Winning Combinations" (page 228) take up many more such dishes, but it helps to use your own preferences and imagination. The broader and more varied your experience with different wines, the better able you are to choose the one that will work best. In the words of John Milton, "Be wise and taste."

Later on, we get more specific about various combinations and their interactions with one another. Before we get into that, however, let me urge you again to remember that tastes and preferences are subjective. The enjoyment of wine is a very individual matter, and not something to be legislated here or anywhere else. Experts can offer useful guidance based on their experience and make suggestions you might not have considered, but the wine in your glass, whether simple or rarefied, can speak for itself—and will if you let it. Wine is such a sociable beverage, a great catalyst in bringing together people from many walks of life. It was made solely to give pleasure, and that pleasure is most rewarding when good bottles are poured in good company. Lifelong friendships have formed over a shared bottle, and I have marveled repeatedly at how certain wines become forever associated with people, places, events.

These connections have often happened quite by accident for me, serendipitous occasions that I relish in retrospect when I come upon the wine again. The wines were not always grand ones, by any means. One that lodged itself in memory years ago was sipped casually in the sun-dappled square of Sancerre, a little hilltop town along the Loire River in France known for its wine of the same name. What made that crisp little quaff so appealing and so memorable? Was it just its simple green-apple freshness, or the delectable lumps of chalk—white chèvre we bought to go with it—or was it the entrancing play of sun and shadow on the square? I cannot say for sure, but to this day the taste of good Sancerre conjures up for me that square, that man, and the sweetness of that moment.

Chapter 2

ORCHESTRATING THE CLASSIC DINNER

▼

To offer wine is the most charming gesture of hospitality,

and a host brings out for his guests the finest he has.

Whether there are four wines or one, the gesture is the same.

ALEXIS LICHINE

*U*ntil the seventies unleashed the wine boom in the United States, the traditional approach to a fine meal was to devise the menu first and then select wines to go with it. With today's wine lovers, however, it often goes the other way around. Special wines are the prime focus of consideration. In fact, they are often the reason the evening is planned in the first place. This does not mean that the food is not important, or that it is in any way slighted; it is just that the menu is selected as a means of showing off the wines to best advantage.

How does such a dinner come about? Sometimes the wine itself demands it. If, for example, I have a fine Meursault that I suspect is at peak of readiness for drinking, or a California Pinot Noir whose progress I want to check out, then I will plan a dinner to include them. More often, however, it simply happens when friends come to town and there is an opportunity to share some good bottles. Sometimes they know a great deal about wine, sometimes nothing at all. While this determines to some extent the wines I will choose, I have found that lack of knowledge rarely keeps people from enjoying a fine wine. Indeed, it is delightful to introduce someone to something new and unexpected.

In the mid-eighties, I attended a dinner in New York so perfectly structured that it could serve as a model for the classic dinner designed around great bottles. It was one of a series of fund-raising dinners held to benefit the New York Public Library, and several of the wines were donated for the occasion. The hosts, Peter and

Nanno Bienstock, used as inspiration for the evening Countess Rostova's glittering dinner described in Tolstoy's *War and Peace*, with its wonderful evocation of two approaches to dining: that of Pierre, who savored every dish and each successive glass of wine, and that of Natasha's German tutor, who ate or drank little but feverishly took notes to send home indignant reports of czarist Russia's excesses.

Since most of the twenty-eight guests at the Bienstocks' were wine lovers, the mood of the evening waxed toward Pierre's "ever-increasing amiability," as we made our way through the succession of wines. The evening began with Champagne and appetizers in the living room, and a grand bottle of bubbly it was—a Methuselah (equivalent of eight bottles) of Moët et Chandon 1973, brisk and elegant, particularly good with the caviar canapés.

About nine o'clock we sat down to dinner, which began with turtle soup accompanied by a glass of Blandy Verdelho, Solera 1880, a semidry Madeira. Old Madeiras are wonderful wines and time had honed and sculpted this one to an amber richness of surprisingly light texture; it was excellent with the soup. The next course was fish, baked striped bass topped with slices of lightly smoked salmon shaped into rosebuds. The choice of wine was a brilliant one. Where there might have been the traditional selection of white Burgundy, white Graves, or California Chardonnay, Peter Bienstock chose instead Taittinger's 1975 Comte de Champagne Rosé. It was dry, quite flavorful, and surprisingly light, a refreshing lift to the palate that was more appropriate at this juncture than something weightier would have been.

It was a superb prelude to the principal wine of the evening, an imperial (equivalent of six liters) of Château Mouton-Rothschild 1934, donated by the château's owner, Baron Philippe de Rothschild. The huge bottle generated considerable comment among the guests. There is always a certain amount of suspense when a rare old bottle of wine is about to be opened. Will it be good, or will it be vinegar? The vintage of 1934 was the best of its decade in Bordeaux, so hopes were high that the wine would be good. All eyes were fixed on the bottle as the cork was eased out (using the screwpull, of course, the corkscrew that could most easily adapt to the oversized bottle neck). The wine was decanted into six gleaming crystal decanters, leaving behind only a few inches of sediment.

All present were amazed at the Mouton's strength and vigor. It took considerable time for it to open up after more than four decades of confinement in the bottle. Little by little the aromas unfolded— spicy fruit, a hint of cedar, oaky vanillins, chocolate. The wine still had plenty of fruit, which had only mellowed with time. It was exquisite to savor with the main course of venison croquettes and breast of mallard.

The 1934 Mouton continued to grow in the glass long after we were into the second red wine of the evening, magnums of Robert Mondavi 1974 Cabernet Sauvignon that were poured with the cheese course. The Cabernet was big, warm, and ripe, although not really ready to drink. Wines in oversized bottles age more slowly because of the greater volume of liquid. Earlier that very day, in fact, I had tasted from regular-size bottles of the 1974 Mondavi, and the wine was superb and perfectly ready. The magnums needed a few more years to reach their full potential, and still do today.

With dessert, a white chocolate and raspberry tart, we were served Château d'Yquem 1967, regarded by many as Yquem's best vintage since 1921. Deep golden in color, it had that incredible balance of powerful but uncloying sweetness that sets Yquem apart from all other Sauternes. After coffee, we adjourned to a selection of old brandies that included a 1929 Armagnac, a 1945 Calvados, and Gaston Briand's Paradis Cognac. About midnight the party began to break up, and it is a fair tribute to the pacing of the evening that no one felt overstuffed or overwined—just full of the mellow well-being that comes from a rarefied combination of good wine, good food, and good company.

Few dinners are as elaborate as that one, although one guest remarked that he would like to dine that way every night. That I would find satiating very quickly indeed. Once in a great while it is terrific, but it is the infrequency of such occasions that makes them special. Dinner today usually consists of four courses: a first course, a main course, cheese and/or salad, and dessert. That is the structure for the menus I have suggested at the end of the chapter. You can always add or omit courses in any meal to suit your own needs.

Planning Ahead

However many courses or wines you plan to have, it takes some careful preparation if the meal is to come off smoothly, with maximum pleasure for all present, including the host. For most wine buffs and collectors, the planning itself is a happy endeavor, since they love to browse among their bottles and see what treasures they can bring out to please their friends. For Dr. Bernard Rhodes, who owns one of the finest private collections of California wines in existence, the planning starts well in advance. He and his wife, Belle, who taught cooking classes for many years, take great pleasure in collaborating on vinous evenings that are eagerly anticipated by their guests. He decides on the wines he wants to serve and together they devise a menu that will give them best support. Like many collectors, Dr. Rhodes sometimes chooses two or three different wines to serve with a particular course rather than additional bottles of the same wine. One memorable evening the wines for the meat course were three 1968 Cabernet Sauvignons—Louis M. Martini Special Selection, Charles Krug Vintage Select, and Heitz Martha's Vineyard. The wines, from one of California's most outstanding vintages, were all superb but in very different ways, stimulating a lively exchange as they opened up and changed with air. We swirled and sniffed and sipped, delighted to discover new facets in each wine as the evening wore on.

Not all of us have such cellars to draw upon, although more and more people are beginning to lay away wines for just such future pleasures. In the meantime, we must rely on what is currently available, and a good wine shop can be a great help. Most of the wine recommendations in this book do not include vintage dates, which in many cases will no longer be available by the time this book is published. Instead, they point more toward a style of wine so that if the wine named is not available, a good wine merchant will be able to suggest alternatives. I recommend that you discuss with your merchant the best vintage years from which to choose.

Before we get into specific match-ups, there are a number of general points to consider in planning a wine dinner. What follow are some of the most important factors to keep in mind as you begin.

First, decide on how many people you will have. A 750-millilieter bottle of wine holds 25.4 ounces and will give six generous servings, or eight of about four ounces (less, possibly, with an old wine that has considerable sediment). To serve more than eight people, therefore, you will need two bottles or more, according to the number of guests.

Since the reason for such get-togethers is to enjoy special wines with friends, most wine lovers prefer to include only as many people as they can accommodate comfortably at the table. A buffet dinner, unless it is a sit-down affair, is not the best setting for serving a succession of fine wines. Juggling a plate on your lap is awkward at best, hardly conducive to appreciating the nuance and complexity of special wines. Make it a sit-down party so that people can enjoy the wines in front of them at their leisure. If your table is not large enough to seat everyone, break up the group and set smaller tables.

Consider the season and choose wines of appropriate weight and texture that not only suit the food but also the temperature. Heady, vigorous reds, for example, are too heavy for hot weather no matter how cool it may be indoors. The ensuing seasonal chapters in this book take this up in greater detail.

Traditionally, the heavier the dish the bigger the wine. However, if an especially fine wine is to occupy center stage, it is generally best to choose a fairly simple, straightforward dish rather than an intricate or elaborate one. This does not mean it has to be bland or dull, by any means. What you want is to give the wine its due, and an overly assertive dish will blunt its impact.

Younger, simpler wines precede those that are older and more mature. To follow up a special bottle with a simpler wine is anticlimactic, and rather unfair to the second wine. One sets up the most dramatic wine of the evening by leading up to it, paving the way, so to speak.

White wines come before red. White wines generally lead up to the principal reds of the meal. White wines that follow reds would be dessert wines or Champagne, for the most part. In certain instances the cheese course offers an exception. If the cheese is Roquefort, Sauternes is a fabulous choice. The best cheese for showing off certain reds—Cabernet, Pommard, Rhônes, for instance, is goat cheese (*chèvre*), a young or briefly aged one, not one that is overripe or ammoniated.

Dry before sweet. There are blatant exceptions to this rule, such as lightly sweet Rieslings served as aperitifs, or Sauternes with the first course. These we explore in more detail later on. Normally, however, dry whites lead up to reds or richer whites.

AN EXCURSION THROUGH A CLASSIC DINNER, COURSE BY COURSE

▼

Aperitifs

Aperitifs are an important consideration for the wine dinner. Coming first, they set the tone and mood for the evening that follows. The term *aperitif* derives from the Latin word *aperire*, which means "to open." As the curtain raiser for the evening, so to speak, aperitifs set up the palate for what is to come. Depending on what is served, they can dull the appetite and anesthetize the palate, or they can serve to stimulate it, awaken the taste buds so that one anticipates the food and the wines to come.

Martinis, highballs, and other potent alcoholic drinks tend to dull the palate, interfering with a full appreciation of the foods and wines to follow. This is not such an important consideration at an informal meal, but for one that is carefully planned with special wines to accompany specially prepared dishes, it is advisable to go light in the beginning by offering wine or lighter alcoholic drinks such as sherry, Lillet, vermouth, or other aperitif wines.

One of the best choices as an aperitif is Champagne, genuine French Champagne or some other sparkling wine. Champagne's lilting ebullience gets any gathering off to a festive start. It is a good icebreaker, too, particularly if there are guests in the group who are meeting one another for the first time. Wine that sparkles is always greeted with delight and has a way of bringing people together quickly and putting them at ease.

One's choice of sparkling wine depends on one's own taste and preference, and Chapter 4 takes up the differences among them in detail. Champagne is an elegant choice for those who prefer its dry, sometimes austere style. More and more, however, people are discovering California's good sparkling wines from such wineries as Domaine Chandon, Piper-Sonoma, Schramsberg, Iron Horse, Château Saint Jean, Domaine Mumm, Roederer Estate, Gloria Ferrer, and Mirassou. They are dry, fresh, and easy to drink. Most of them are less expensive than French Champagne, although top blends like Schramsberg Reserve cost as much as any vintage Champagne.

Serving Champagne throughout a meal is a romantic idea in the minds of many people, but for me this is too much of a good thing, especially at a meal of several courses. An excess of effervescence has a way of becoming uncomfortably indigestible after a while. Producers of sparkling wines and Champagnes like to promote the notion of all-Champagne meals. Yet even in the Champagne region of France it is rarely done, and then usually to prove the questionable point that Champagne goes with anything and everything. When the Champenois entertain, the meal invariably begins and ends with Champagne, but with a main course of meat they generally serve Bordeaux. In a multicourse meal, Champagne can certainly accompany certain courses, even the main course, where it will often serve to lighten a rather heavy dish. I'm reminded of a dinner prepared by Nicole Routhier, author of *The Cooking of Vietnam*, that matched Veuve Clicquot Brut Rosé with a spicy beef stew—an imaginative combination that worked superbly.

For a variation on the Champagne theme, pour a drop or two of crème de cassis (black currant liqueur) into a flute-shaped Champagne glass (referred to simply as a flute), then add the wine. This increasingly popular drink is known as a Kir Royal (see page 160 for recipe). The cassis turns the drink into a delightful pink froth. You must determine how much cassis to use; more than a couple of drops will make the drink too sweet and *very* pink indeed. One of my favorite preprandials is Champagne Cocktail, a bracing start when made correctly (page 161).

Not everyone likes sparkling wines, so always be sure to have something else on hand. Another white wine would probably be a safe choice, but do not settle for the usual jug white or bar white that people can get anywhere. There are too many good white wines from which to choose. Consider, however, that one may not want to begin with a bone-dry wine, like Muscadet or Alsace Riesling. These wines can be a little forbidding early in the evening and are perhaps better with the first course. People often claim they like only dry wine, but I have found that when I serve a German *Kabinett* or *Spätlese*, people enjoy it very much, despite the fact that it has a touch of sweetness. They are often quite surprised to discover something delightful that they had overlooked.

Another good category to consider for aperitifs is white wine made from red grapes—either the dry *vin gris*, or Pinot Noir Blanc, white Zinfandel, or Cabernet Blanc. These wines are usually not fully dry, but neither are they really sweet. I have often started with a Blanc de Pinot Noir, particularly in the summer, because it is especially light—only 11 percent alcohol—and delightfully refreshing.

SERVING DRY SHERRY

In Spain, the delectable little appetizers known as *tapas* are always accompanied by dry sherry. *Tapas* evolved as something to soak up alcohol and assuage stimulated gastric juices. As a fortified wine, sherry can be anywhere from 16 to 20 percent alcohol. Dry sherries like fino or manzanilla are the lighest in body and the usual choice for these appetizers in Spain, but amontillado, with its mildly sweet, nutty flavors, is also a good one. Traditionally, sherry was served straight up in small glasses known as *copitas*. Today, it is often served on the rocks, even with a twist of lemon, though it seems something of a shame to dilute the taste of fine sherry in this way. Fino and manzanilla are best chilled, and will keep better if refrigerated after opening.

Other choices for before dinner are the aromatic fortified wines like vermouth, both sweet and dry, Campari, Lillet, Dubonnet, and others. Many of them, such as Punt e Mes, Campari, or Amer Picon, are quite bitter, too much so for some people. It is the quinine and bitter herbs that provide the bite; served *natur* they would stun rather than quicken the palate, so they are generally served chilled with a liberal splash of soda and lemon or orange zest, either straight up or on the rocks.

The period of aperitifs should not be too long. One or two drinks is about right. An extended period of before-dinner drinks is the great villain leading to overindulgence. On an empty stomach, alcohol goes right into the bloodstream and once there it is too late to remedy. Light accompaniments to aperitifs are best if the dinner to follow consists of several courses, but they should be based on some sort of protein, which slows the rate of alcohol absorption. Nuts, cheese, fish, eggs, and meat are all good choices.

The First Course

The menu ideas in the first five chapters always include wine suggestions for the first course unless it happens to be soup. Some people prefer not to have wine with soup because it seems an excess of liquids, and the textures do not always enhance one another. Perhaps that is why the richer fortified wines like sherry or Madeira became traditional with consommés and seafood bisques. You may pour the wine in the soup, if you like. That, too, is traditional. If the wine is a good or rare one, however, like the Madeira at the Bienstock dinner, it may be more enjoyable to drink it.

Remember that the wine for the first course sets the stage for the wine to follow. A light white wine would precede a rich white Burgundy or California Chardonnay that might be served with a main course of fish or veal. If the main course is meat and red wine, the first course may well be fish, such as coquilles Saint Jacques with its cream sauce or quenelles in a *beurre blanc* or Champagne sauce; here, one of the bigger whites is entirely appropriate.

One of the most dramatic pairings in wine and food is foie gras with Sauternes, the luscious sweet wine from the Sauternes district of Bordeaux in France. It is a marriage of such unctuous richness that you would expect the two to fight hideously or cancel each other out. On the contrary, it is one of those sublime matches that one must experience to appreciate. The sweetness of the wine, with its high degree of acidity, is the perfect foil for the smooth, rich liver paste. In Alsace, home of outstanding foie gras, a rich Gewürztraminer, such as one labeled *vendange tardive* (late harvest), is served with the dish. It has the character and strength to accommodate the richness of the pâté, but the combination is less sensuous than the match with Sauternes.

These forceful wines should only be served at this juncture in the meal if they are to precede fairly sizable reds like Cabernet Sauvignon, Bordeaux, full-bodied Burgundies, or the like. The powerful sweetness would destroy any white wine that followed.

Rieslings and Gewürztraminers are excellent with other sorts of pâté, especially country pâtés or those with pungent flavoring. Several other wines will suit just as well, however, including light reds like Beaujolais or Napa Gamay, with its faint sweetness and high acidity. Vouvray is another good choice with meat pâté.

Fish pâtés are generally quite delicate in flavor. Dry Riesling or a German *Kabinett* suits the subtleties quite well when there is no accompanying sauce, such as a piquant green sauce or a rich mayonnaise. With a sauce, something more assertive is called for, such as Muscadet, Sancerre, or Mâcon-Villages. Use similar guidelines for vegetable pâtés, which also tend to be fairly mild.

The Main Course

At most wine dinners, the featured wine of the evening is served either with the main course or the cheese course. If it is a white wine, a fine Burgundy or Chardonnay, then the main course will most likely be fish, although it could also be something like veal or chicken breasts in a cream sauce. If the wine is red, a simple but elegant meat dish is the best choice, something on the order of roast lamb, beef, or gamebirds.

Two or more bottles may be needed for the main course, depending on the number of guests. You can serve two bottles of the same wine, and many people do. Or, as mentioned earlier, you can serve different wines. It is amusing to serve two different wines of the same vintage—two Médoc châteaux, for example, or two California Cabernets. The wines must be compatible, of course, from the same year or the same region, and reasonably close in style. You would not serve a Bordeaux and a Burgundy at the same time, but two Bordeaux from different châteaux could be an intriguing match, or two different California Cabernets. Let us say you have two wines from different parts of Bordeaux: Château Pichon-Lalande from the Médoc and Domaine de Chevalier from Graves. Pour the two wines simultaneously but taste the Pichon first. Note its deep, graceful fruit, rather narrowly defined, as is typical of wines from the village of Pauillac. Then taste the Graves. It is more supple, with broader flavors that seem nearer the surface, more accessible than the Pichon; yet they are no less interesting for that. The character has a certain mineral accent that makes it earthier than the Pauillac but not coarse.

There are similar pathways of flavor to search for in California Cabernets from different regions—say, Stag's Leap or Caymus from Napa Valley and Jordan from Alexander Valley or one of the stunning proprietary blends such as Carmenet, Dominus, Opus One, Rubicon, or Clos du Val Reserve. The better the wines and the vintage, the more they are likely to reveal, especially if they have had a generous amount of time to develop. Young Bordeaux or Cabernet Sauvignon that is only three or four years old may show enormous potential for the future, but time alone can open up the labyrinths of flavor within them. The better ones are just starting to show their stuff after eight or ten years.

It is quite common to serve both a Bordeaux and a Cabernet, and such comparisons are fun if done in the right spirit, which is *not* to have them compete with one another, but simply to explore inherently different styles.

Usually, if different vintages are involved, they go with different courses, the younger one with the main course, the older with the cheese. There are exceptions to consider. If I were serving a Bordeaux from 1978 and one from 1986, I might well serve the older wine first, since 1986 Bordeaux were much bigger and more powerful wines than those from 1978. The younger wine, however, would probably need a fairly flavorful cheese like farmhouse Cheddar or aged Cantal.

Salad and Cheese

These courses are often combined. This is perfectly acceptable practice, particularly if the cheese is *chèvre*, which works so well with salad greens. It creates a bit of a problem with wine, however, though I have found one wine that works: very young Orvieto Classico, no more than a year old. The high acidity of vinegar will make most wines taste flat and dull, unless they are fairly acidic themselves, like Orvieto or Sauvignon Blanc. I consider the salad course, if I include one, a pause in the meal and serve it without wine as a sort of palate refresher. It should be lightly dressed, with little or no vinegar, which would fight the wines. I often use lemon juice as a substitute for vinegar, and some wine connoisseurs recommend another alternative—a spot of cognac. Interestingly, balsamic vinegar does not clash as harshly with wine as do other vinegars, but restraint is advised.

Cheese and wine, it is often said, were made for each other. Truly, they are the most convivial of companions, with some exceptions, such as overly ripened Brie or Gorgonzola, which are too pungent for any wine. More often cheese and wine bring out the best in each other. In fact, nothing is better suited for certain fine, old wines than a savory, but not too savory, cheese.

Depending on the structure of the dinner as a whole, the cheese course can be a crucial one. For me, as for many wine lovers, no meal is really complete or satisfying unless it includes a solid red wine. Thus, if I am serving fish as the main course, I usually include a cheese course to accommodate the red wine I want to serve. An attractive cheese board and a special wine give the meal a boost at this point. By this time, the guests are relaxed and ready for new tastes—*if* they have not been overburdened by too much beforehand. I try to keep preceding courses reasonably light if I am offering cheeses, especially if there are several.

One superb cheese can be quite enough if it is just right, such as a creamy Brie *fermier* or the piquant-flavored Burgundian soft cheese Époisses, which is one of my favorites. Strong-flavored cheeses can overpower wine. Take care, for instance, with ripe soft-ripened cheeses (Brie, Camembert); ammoniated rinds will ruin wine. Blue cheeses pose special problems sometimes. Rich, mellow Stilton can go nicely with a strong red, but it is best, I think, with a good port, either vintage or ruby. Roquefort is too strong for almost any wine, except one. Sauternes with Roquefort is one of the most exciting combinations in the realm of wine and food. This must sound bizarre to anyone who has not tried it, but the viscous sweetness of the wine and the sharpness of the sheep's milk blue unite to create a marriage made in heaven: it is truly blissful. Sweet wines will go with other blue cheeses as well, including Gorgonzola, Bleu de Bressc, Fourme d'Ambert, Danish blues, and other creamy blues. Blue Cheshire, however, is better with claret or port because of the Cheshire-like flavor of the basic cheese.

If there are to be several cheeses, they should show contrasts in flavor, texture, and appearance that will appeal to the eye and the palate. For example, it would not be good to serve Port Salut, Doux de Montagne, and Gouda all at once. Basically, these cheeses have the same texture, mild flavor, and color. It would be more interesting to include a savory cheese, such as aged Cheddar or Asiago, a creamy cheese like Camembert, perhaps a *chèvre* in a distinctive log or pyramid shape, and a blue that is not overly sharp.

Dessert

Dessert is extremely important to most people, but I must confess that it is not for me. Once it is set in front of me, I may find it an irresistible temptation. In restaurants, I rarely have it, mainly because I have had enough to eat, but frequently also because I want to enjoy the lingering aftertaste of a good wine. Dessert wine, however, is something else again. There are some wonderful ones. At dinner parties I usually serve a simple dessert—sorbet, a fruit tart, or perhaps cake. Syrupy sweet desserts such as rich creams or pies will smother most sweet wines. Dessert wines like Sauternes, late-harvest Rieslings, or sweet Moscatos are luscious by themselves, with maybe a cookie or two. Chilled and sweet, they are also an especially nice way to cap a summer meal. Restaurants are offering more dessert wines, ports, and sherries by the glass, and it is a good way to get to know some of them.

Giving the sated palate an uplift is the reason for serving sparkling wines after dinner, and I quite like them as a change of pace. Dry Champagne or sparkling wines may be too austere for after dinner, particularly if they are served with a light cake. Extra dry Champagne is a better choice with cake and light sweet bubbly is making a comeback. Cliquot's Demi-Sec is ravishing. Schramsberg and Sharffenberger make a dessert Champagne (California) called Crémant that is marvelous with fruit mousses or fresh raspberries.

Postprandials

It is hospitable to offer after-dinner drinks, either vintage port or brandies. Once upon a time it would have been remiss not to do so, but nowadays the thoughtful host will keep in mind the guests' destination and have some concern that they get there safely. Encourage any drivers in the group to drink lightly or not at all by having soda, mineral water, or nonalcohol beer or wine on hand. In any case, after-dinner drinks should be wine-based rather than grain-based. Grape and grain do not mix well together, and if anything will promote a hangover, that combination surely will.

The menus suggested for the classic wine dinner are more elaborate than those in later chapters, where suggestions for more casual meals like picnics, barbecues, and weekend brunches are included. Extra courses may be added for more elegant occasions, of course, or courses omitted for simpler entertaining.

MENUS FOR CLASSIC DINNERS

I.

Caviar	**Taittinger's Blanc de Blancs**
Bay Scallops with Shallots	**Savennières**
Roast Leg of Lamb Rosemary **Broiled Tomatoes** **Green Beans with Celery, Almonds, and Garlic**	**Bordeaux (Médoc)**
Roquefort	**Sauternes**

MENU NOTES: Blanc de Blancs Champagne, with its bright, zingy fruit, has the edge over fuller-bodied Champagnes with caviar for my taste; others prefer the richer styles like Krug Grande Cuvée, but any dry white wine will do—as long as it sparkles. Shellfish and Sauvignon Blanc generally blend superbly with one another. As one of the more delicate shellfish, scallops need a less assertive dry white. Savennières, made from Chenin Blanc, has the character to handle the shallots without overwhelming the scallops, especially if the wine is three or four years old. Lamb with rosemary is a classic with firm-flavored Médoc from Pauillac or Saint Julien. An equally good choice would be Napa Valley Cabernet, particularly one of those from the Rutherford area. Roquefort and Sauternes are a thrilling match.

II.

Savories	MANZANILLA

Carrot Soup	

Braised Breast of Pheasant	CHAMBOLLE-MUSIGNY
Brussels Sprouts with Sesame	
Red Peppers with Garlic and Coriander	

Stilton	PORT
Seasonal Fruit	

MENU NOTES: With manzanilla, a dry sherry, you might serve such savories as salted almonds, olives, smoked oysters, or smoked salmon. The carrot soup needs no wine, although an off-dry Riesling from the Rhine could accompany it. Chambolle-Musigny is one of the more graceful red Burgundies from the Côte de Nuits, an excellent match for gamebirds. Other possibilities: Clos de la Roche, Volnay, Pernand-Vergelesses, Saintsbury Pinot Noir, or an Oregon Pinot Noir Reserve. Fonseca Bin 27 is one of the best ruby ports, a fine match with Stilton. A not-quite-mature vintage port, such as 1977 or 1983, would also work, but be sure to decant it (pages 195–96).

III.

Fresh *Chèvres* and Crudités	SANCERRE

Grilled Fresh Tuna New Potatoes with Herb Butter Green Salad	CALIFORNIA MERLOT

Cheeses: Brie, Cantal, Langres	NUITS-SAINT-GEORGES
Fresh Strawberries with Kirsch	ESPRESSO

MENU NOTES: Crudités such as celery sticks, scallions, red pepper, carrots, and broccoli are quite good with fresh young goat cheese, which is soft enough to use as a dip; soften it with a little yogurt if necessary. Sancerre is superb with *chèvre*. Red-meat tuna will overwhelm most white wines, but a supple Merlot such as St. Francis, J. Carey, or Inglenook would suit it handsomely. Another good choice would be a light Rhône such as Côtes du Ventoux. The cheeses, two soft and one firm (Cantal), are among those that would complement the red Burgundy from Nuits-Saint-Georges.

IV.

Stuffed Mushroom Canapés	Dry Vermouth on the Rocks
Cucumber-Yogurt Soup	
Steamed Lobster **Saffron Rice with June Peas**	California Chardonnay
Pears with Sagablu Cheese	Late-Harvest Gewürztraminer Espresso, hot or iced

MENU NOTES: This summer menu is fairly self-explanatory. A vermouth drink with a little more pizzazz is the Americano (see recipe on pages 162–63). Cucumber-yogurt soup makes a good hot-weather refresher; add puréed zucchini to give it a greener, cooler look, if you like. The flavor and texture of lobster needs a crisp but full-bodied Chardonnay, such as Trefethen or Clos du Bois Calcaire. A Chablis *grand cru* is a good alternative. If there is any sauce served with the lobster, one of the richer white Burgundies, such as Puligny-Montrachet, would be a better choice than Chablis. Sagablu is a creamy Danish blue cheese that is delectable with late-harvest Gewürztraminer or Riesling.

Cherry Tomatoes Stuffed with Taramosalata	APERITIFS
Grilled Shrimp on Skewers **Pork and Veal Pâté** **Paupiettes of Sole** **Spinach Ravioli**	CHÂTEAU CARBONNIEUX GRAVES BLANC
Roast Prime Rib of Beef	CABERNET SAUVIGNON RESERVE OR CALIFORNIA PINOT NOIR
Sweetbreads Bonne Femme* **Zucchini Gratin** **Hot Breads**	
Cheeses: Camembert, Montrachet *Chèvre*, Double Gloucester	
Glazed Mango Slices **Tiny Mocha Eclairs**	ESPRESSO COGNAC

MENU NOTES: The tomatoes and shrimp are appetizers to go with aperitifs before dinner. Taramosalata is a creamy paste of salmon roe. If there are twelve or more guests, try to have available a selection of aperitifs—Lillet, Campari, vermouth, as well as white wine such as Mâcon or Beaujolais Blanc. At dinner, guests may serve themselves from the buffet, but the wines should be served at table, with three wineglasses at each place setting. Plates should be removed after the pâté and sole, when guests return to the

*See M. F. K. Fisher's *With Bold Knife and Fork.*

buffet for the main course. They may return again for cheese, or you can pass the cheese board around the table after the main course is finished.

Château Carbonnieux is a dry white Graves suggested mainly for the sole, but since it is a blend of Sémillon and Sauvignon Blanc, it can also accompany pâté. Reserve Cabernet is a classic match with prime rib, as Pinot Noir is with sweetbreads, but a richer Pinot Noir such as Robert Mondavi Reserve, Beaulieu Carneros, or Sinskey could handle both meats. Either wine could also continue with the cheese, or you could turn to a different red such as Crozes-Hermitage.

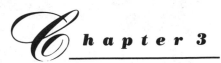

SAVORING AUTUMN'S BOUNTY

▼

The covered-in courtyard, lit by arc-lamps, rang with the clangour of voices, wheels and heavily shod feet, for the forty or so vintagers of the estate were on their way down to their repast, bringing in with them their aroma of male vigour and the juices of the wine.

COLETTE IN BEAUJOLAIS, *The Blue Lantern*, 1947

*I*s there a seasonal aspect to wine? you may well ask. For a great many wines, the answer is no. Certainly we do not confine light reds and white wines to summer, although we tend to have them more often during that season. There are also those who break tradition completely and drink only white wine, or only red wine, no matter what food is being served. For wine enthusiasts, however, the time of year plays an important role when choosing wine.

The start of a new season always prods my palate a bit. The first rattle of dry leaves across the pavement in autumn wakes in me, as it must in many wine lovers, the longing to savor a good solid red wine like Bordeaux or Cabernet Sauvignon or Hermitage, wines that are really not appropriate for hot weather. The yearning sets me to thinking of menus for my first autumn dinner party.

Usually my choice for the main course is lamb, since I long for a good roast that will set off the red I have in mind. This is the time of year when I am most eager to mount a dinner like the ones described in the previous chapter, when I can bring out some of the wines I have ignored during the summer months when foods and wines were lighter and simpler.

Autumn is the time for the last alfresco outings of the year, such as picnics, harvest dinners, and autumn barbecues—unless you are given to outdoor forays in winter. Autumn is also the harvest season, and for winegrowers and winemakers it is the climax of the year, the culmination of all their efforts since the start of the growing season in early spring. There is always an electric feeling in the fall, when the air takes on a crisp chill in the evening but the days are still warm and sunny. This time of year always finds me in one or another of the world's wine regions, and it is an exciting time to be there. Wine country in autumn hums with activity as the harvest gets under way. Winegrowers, winemakers, even casual tourists get caught up in the extra excitement that charges the atmosphere. It is a tense time, but an exhilarating one as the new vintage is harvested and the air is sweet with the scent of ripe grapes.

Harvest—or "crush," as those involved call it—is also an incredibly arduous time. Some wineries operate around the clock. If the chardonnay is at perfect ripeness for picking, then it must be taken at just the right moment, even if that happens to be three o'clock in the morning. Mechanical harvesters now enable winegrowers to pick at any time of day or night, when the grapes are at peak ripeness. When the gondolas full of grapes line up at the crushing pad at the winery, the cellar crew must be there to weigh them in and get the grapes ready for fermentation. Sleep becomes a luxury grabbed when a slack in the momentum permits. In light of all the hard work and time pressure, it is not surprising that when it is all over—somewhere between the end of September and the end of October—the vintners want to celebrate. Harvest dinners are indeed a celebration, especially in years when the vintage is a good one.

A few years ago I had the pleasure of attending a harvest dinner at Clinton Vineyards near Poughkeepsie, New York. Owner Ben Feder grows seyval blanc, a white French-American hybrid grape variety, at his fourteen-acre vineyard some ninety minutes north of New York City. Each September Clinton's grape pickers are friends and neighbors who come to help out on weekends for the sheer love of it—and also for the harvest feasts. There are grand feeds for hungry vineyard workers at midday and again in the evening. It is a time of great camaraderie and high-spirited fun.

The year I was there French chef Étienne Merle, owner of Le Cochon Rouge in Syracuse, had come down to handle the two spit-roasted lambs that were the mainstay of the dinner. They turned slowly over open fires on the lawn outside the winery. Over coals in a large barbecue nearby, ears of fresh local corn roasted, still in the shuck. We had our pick of the stack and stood in the late-afternoon sun stripping back the charred husks and eating the corn right on the spot. It was so fresh and succulent that it needed nothing on it, though there were pots of soft butter to slather on for those who wanted it.

The meal itself took place in a large, two-level barnlike room behind the winery fermentation area. It started with pasta shells in pesto sauce, made with fresh basil from Cathy Feder's kitchen garden. There was plenty of Clinton Vineyards Seyval Blanc to wash it down, and the dry, crisp white was perfect with it. (Who says they can't make good wine east of the Rockies? Only those who have not had the right ones.)

With the lamb we had a sound Italian red wine from the Valtellina district in northern Italy. It was simple but sturdy and full-bodied. Somehow, lamb grilled over live coals has a heartier flavor than lamb roasted in the oven. For that reason, it can take a heartier wine than the classic well-aged Bordeaux or California Cabernet that is traditionally served with roast lamb. Several Italian reds suit the situation, certainly any of the reds from the Valtellina, with their extravagantly operatic names—Grumello, Inferno, Sassella—are excellent choices. One of the sturdier California Cabernets would have made an equally fine choice, such as Pedroncelli, Louis M. Martini Rosso, Burgess, or Sterling Three Palms.

I had brought along a couple of bottles of Bordeaux to try with Ben Feder that evening and Étienne had brought down from upstate a new goat cheese (now widely known on the East Coast) made by an outfit called the Goat Folks. The cheese was fresh and delicate, delicious with the red wine. The party grew friendlier and louder and there was much traffic between tables as people exchanged stories and jokes about the day's work. Warmed and nourished by the good food and wine, the camaraderie in the big room soon swelled to a din that reverberated to the rafters. The group all had worked hard and now they played hard. It is a philosophy inherent to most wine regions, I have found, one of the things that makes them so dynamic and appealing.

Out in California, good eating does not stop at crush time, despite the exhaustive pace and irregular hours that hold sway. Entertaining gets quite lavish, in fact, and at some wineries the hardworking cellar crew eat very well indeed. At Joseph Phelps Vineyard in Napa Valley, for instance, Joe Phelps himself has been known to don a chef's apron and pitch in to help prepare "crew dinners" in the winery's well-equipped kitchen. The meals are hearty ones and the flow of wine is liberal, but it is needed for the long night's work.

Over at Robert Mondavi Winery in Oakville, the Great Chef program is in full swing as noted chefs such as Paul Bocuse, Joel Robuchon, Julia Child, Anne Rosenzweig, and a host of new American chefs demonstrate their techniques to avid students. The highlight of each day is dinner in the winery's Harvest Room, which opens onto one of the Mondavis's Cabernet vineyards. It is an impressive room, vast and spacious, designed in the style of the early California missions. In the evening, lit with candles, flickering shadows create an atmosphere that recalls the days of the *californios* who first settled California and left everywhere the mark of their Spanish heritage.

Many California wineries now emphasize the connection between wine and food. Karen Keehn of McDowell Vineyards in Mendocino has long experimented with various combinations, which she reports in McDowell's newsletter. Beringer Vineyards operates a fabulous School for American Chefs in Napa Valley, with Madeleine Kamman at the helm. "What is wine without food?" she asks. "In France, the two are inseparable, so I feel quite at home in this wine valley." Fetzer's Valley Oaks Wine and Food Center in Mendocino features a lush organic garden that supplies vegetables, herbs, and fruits for its wine and food events and the Chef's Kitchen in Hopland. Sterling Vineyards opened a Wine and Food Center for training restaurateurs and wait staff in 1989. Most wineries today, in fact, offer food suggestions, recipes, and other gastronomic tidbits.

Iron Horse Vineyards in the Russian Valley of Sonoma takes harvest cooking a step further and brings in a "crush cook" each fall. Ann Clark, a talented cook from Austin, Texas, started the tradition in the early eighties. More recently, young chefs from the Culinary Institute in San Francisco man the grill and ovens. Invited guests meet for lunch in the latticed gazebo that overlooks the vineyards of Iron Horse. Inside are two long wooden tables and benches, and a table at the far end is laden with food. Owners Barry and Audrey Sterling pour out Iron Horse Brut or Blanc de Blancs as aperitifs. The sumptuous luncheon fare may range from braised breast of pheasant to *pissaladière* (provençal tomato-onion tart) or fresh Pacific salmon, but it is invariably delectable and so beautiful to look at that people hesitate—only briefly, however—to plunge in and devour it.

After an hour or so, an immense sense of relaxed well-being takes over. Often I have sat here, or in similar vineyard settings, and let the timeless beauty of the vine-covered hills work their magic. The vineyards, still green, lush, and graceful, have just yielded up the abundance of their promise. They will turn golden, red, and purple before the leaves fall, leaving a tangle of canes that must be trimmed and pruned for next year's growth. It is a sight that evokes a deep sense of nature's continuity, the heartbeat of a planet that goes about its business with its own rhythm and certainty, quite beyond the frenzied scurry of the beings who people it. Here, the "getting and spending" at work in the rest of the world seem very remote indeed.

Autumn Picnics

Another fall institution is the tailgate picnic. Such picnics never really went out of fashion—they have only become more elegant and possibly more compact with the advent of smaller station wagons. These days they are just as likely to be seen at the polo field, since polo is an increasingly popular spectator sport in many parts of the country. You have wide choices of wines for picnics, because the occasion can be as casual or as fancy as you want it to be. The wines can be anything from Champagne to White Zinfandel, depending solely on your taste; however, picnic time is not the moment for a wine that needs serious attention. There are likely to be too many other distractions and a great deal of noise as well: on a lighthearted occasion such as this a serious wine simply will not do. If you want to be tony, choose Champagne or a good sparkling wine like Bouvet Brut, Piper-Sonoma Brut, or Codorníu Blanc de Blancs.

This occasion, when the food is likely to involve many different flavors, could also be a perfect one for rosé, winedom's most overlooked wine. I keep hoping for a revolution in the realm of rosé—that winemakers will see the light and make them drier. I am glad to see inklings of evidence in the *vin gris* wines of Bonny Doon, Saintsbury, and Sanford. *Vin gris* (literally translated as "gray wine") is a term coined in Burgundy for the pale tint of wines made from red grapes. They are not the same as the paler pinks we now refer to as blush wines, mostly white Zinfandel, which are sweet. *Vin gris* is dry, and may it ever remain so. A good dry rosé goes well with a number of picnic foods, including smoked salmon, pâté, roast chicken, or ham, and such side dishes as baked beans, potato salad, quiche, and other casual fare. I choose a rosé for foods like these when I want something that is sturdier than white wine, yet still crisp and refreshing because it is chilled.

Unless you favor the lightly sweet rosés, choose drier styles like the Provençal rosés of Tavel or Domaine Tempier or Richeaume. Italian rosés are usually dry and there are some charming ones, such as Chiaretto del Garda, which comes from the shores of Lake Garda, not far from Verona. Another is Castel del Monte Rosa (*rosato* is Italian for rosé), and Rosa del Golfo from the south. A particular favorite of mine is Vinruspo, made at the Capezzana estate in Tuscany. (Capezzana is known mostly for its fine red wine, Carmignano.) Vinruspo is an excellent rosé, though made in limited quantities. It is fresh, dry, and delightfully brisk, very good with cold Italian ham or with sausage. According to Count Ugo Buonocossi, who owns Capezzana, there is a story behind the Vinruspo name. The term *ruspo* means "robbed." It seems that in earlier days the grape pickers would haul the last cart of grapes home overnight, to be delivered next morning to the winery. Before they set off, however, they would siphon off a demijohn or so of juice for themselves, setting it aside to ferment slowly. Overnight, the juice would absorb a blush of color from the skins, where all the color pigments reside, and the resulting wine was rosé.

Another good choice for picnics is white Zinfandel or Zinfandel Rosé, although the latter can be rather sweet. It is a good idea to try a couple of these wines ahead of time so that you know which style you are getting—sweet or dry. White Zinfandel and other blush wines really took off in the eighties. Sales show faint signs of waning but blush wines are undoubtedly here to stay. Some of the better ones are made by Buehler, Louis M. Martine, DeLoach, Zaca Mesa, and Stevenot, but others are worth exploring. Pedroncelli and Concannon both make good Zinfandel rosés.

The Savor of Sausage

Another taste I yearn for in autumn is that of sausage. A weekend brunch or Sunday supper of sautéed boudin blanc, bratwurst, or bauenwurst, served with sauerkraut or warm potato salad, is a great autumn favorite of mine. *Choucroute garnie alsacienne* is the very apotheosis of sausage and I adore it, even though I do not permit myself to have it too often. In Alsace, the natives have their "fix" of *choucroute* once a week at least. If you travel there (and I highly recommend it as one of the most charming wine regions anywhere), pay a visit to La Maison des Tanneurs in Strasbourg. *Choucroute garnie* is the house specialty and a fabulous rendition it is. It comes on a trencher-size plate with a mound of steaming sauerkraut, cooked the way it should be with a dry Alsace Riesling. The *garnie* is some "garnish" indeed: local sausages of several different types—cervelat, knockwurst, blood sausage, pork sausage, sausages bland and piquant. *Choucroute* is a nosher's paradise, enormously filling but gloriously satisfying, rather the way cassoulet is, a dish I consider more of a winter specialty.

Many of the lighter wines, white or red, go with sausage dishes, but by all means consider the wine served with the dish in its native land. In Alsace, for example, the Alsatians almost invariably drink their wonderful dry Riesling with *choucroute*, especially since the sauerkraut is cooked in it. Sylvaner and Pinot Blanc, two other good Alsace wines, are lower in acidity and thus too mild for the piquant flavors of the dish. Gewürztraminer is too strong, in my view, though some prefer it. Along the Loire, sausage dishes are accompanied by either the light wines of the Touraine like dry Vouvray, or such Loire Valley reds as Saumur-Champigny, which is fruity like *Cru* Beaujolais, or sturdier Chinon and Bourgueil.

My favorite wine with sausage is Beaujolais. In the Beaujolais region—and the gastronomic center of nearby Lyon—one of the most popular local dishes is *saucisson chaud à la lyonnaise*, poached or grilled pork sausage with hot potato salad. In this part of France, sausage dishes are commonly served with one of the Beaujolais, either simple Beaujolais or Beaujolais-Villages that are best lightly chilled, or the more substantial wines that are named for the communes where they are grown—such as Brouilly, Morgon, Juliénas, Saint-Amour. In autumn, however, the wine in Lyon is most likely to be Beaujolais *nouveau*, the new wine of the just-completed harvest.

The third Thursday in November, the first day the wine can be sold legally, has become an international festival of sorts in capitals throughout the world. *Nouveau*mania, some call it, and enormous hype surrounds the wine's arrival in Paris, New York, London, Chicago, San Francisco, and Los Angeles. There is no mystery to its popularity in good vintages, when the wine is soft, fruity, and luscious, delightfully refreshing when it is lightly chilled, as it should be to enhance the fruit. Before World War II, few had ever heard of Beaujolais *nouveau* or *primeur* (both terms are used for the first wine drawn from the vat). Its original purpose was to provide the locals with a fresh quaff to drink while the wine of the new vintage settled and matured for a few months. It was scarcely more than a rosé in those days, trucked by the barrel into Lyon restaurants where it was served in carafes. Somewhere along the line it became the smart drink in Paris cafés and eventually began to attract a huge following. Nowadays, over 50 percent of the crop is made into *nouveau*. The Beaujolais shippers take it quite seriously and some of the exported wines are sturdier than they used to be.

For the most part, however, the charm of *nouveau* is short-lived.

Within a few months its cherubic fruit starts to fade, leaving the wine a bit sharp and acidic. When Beaujolais *de l'année*, as the wine of the current vintage is called in France, arrives, usually in spring following the vintage, the *nouveau* is "retired"—if there is any left—and the regular wine takes its place. I have been in homes in this country where I saw bottles of *nouveau* that were two or three years old, which must have been quite disappointing when the people finally got around to drinking them. They must wonder what all the fuss is about. To enjoy Beaujolais *nouveau* at its best, drink it within three to six months of the harvest.

Some people are surprised to learn that wines labeled Fleurie or Brouilly or Moulin-à-Vent are actually Beaujolais. There are nine of these wines, however, and ardent Beaujolais fans (of whom I am one) claim to have their favorites. The wines come from a string of quaint villages that stretch across the higher slopes of the Beaujolais hills. Like all Beaujolais, they are made from the gamay grape. Even though each wine has its own character, in some years the differences are not very great. "The differences mostly have to do with what the winemaker chooses to emphasize," says Michel Brun, right-hand man of Georges Duboeuf, the region's largest shipper. "Brouilly and Côte de Brouilly are the lightest. Juliénas has the heartiest fruit. Morgon is the hard one that usually lasts the longest. Moulin-à-Vent is the biggest and fullest—in years like 1989 it was almost a light Burgundy."

"Chiroubles is the archetypical Beaujolais," says another shipper, Didier Mommessin. "Juliénas may have deeper fruit, Fleurie more perfume, but Chiroubles is the prettiest, the one with freshest fruit and its own distinct personality. It is the one that made Beaujolais's reputation. That, of course, is in good years, when the sun is generous. In poorer years it is thinner and not as good as the others." Several of the ten villages of the upper Beaujolais have their own little *caveau*, or tasting grotto, where one may sample the local wine. The villages are not very far apart from one another. You can easily drive from Saint-Amour at the northern end to Brouilly, the southernmost commune, in half a day, stopping for lunch at a local restaurant. It is an easy side trip from Mâcon or Lyon, and well worth a detour.

Several California wineries make an appealing Beaujolais-style wine from gamay beaujolais (actually one of the lighter clones of pinot noir) or from Napa Gamay, sometimes a blend of the two. Wineries like Glen Ellen, Beringer, Preston, Fetzer, J. Lohr, Robert Pecota and others produce very appealing light reds that, like Beaujolais, are best lightly chilled. Charles F. Shaw, who set out expressly to produce *cru*-style Beaujolais in Napa Valley, comes remarkably close in some vintages with a full-bodied Napa Gamay that is reminiscent of Fleurie or Saint-Amour.

Italy also has an abundance of sausage, regional specialties served with native wines, such everyday reds as simple Chianti, Barbera, Dolcetto d'Alba, and Rubesco. Simple Chianti is a wine of medium weight and body, but the others, particularly Barbera and Dolcetto, are more robust than Beaujolais; they are darker in color and have a chewier texture of fruit and tannin, which makes them a good match for dishes like sausage and peppers or sausage pizza. However, something lighter and chillable, like Lambrusco, is better with the snappiness of pepperoni pizza. In Emilia-Romagna, the local dry Lambrusco goes superbly with the native specialty known as *zampone*, a pig's-foot sausage. Dry Lambrusco is light and fruity, quite different from the sweet Lambruscos exported to the United States. It is excellent with the rich sausage and illustrates how suitable chillable reds or dry rosés can be with sausage dishes. Here again, the Provençal rosés come to mind, as long as they are young and fresh. Look for one no older than a year or two.

Duck and Rabbit

I also like to serve duck and rabbit dishes in autumn. There are so many wonderful dishes made with duck, starting with duck pâté. Dry Gewürztraminer goes very well with duck liver pâté, which needs a crisp, flavorful wine to offset the richness of the liver. The wine is good with many Oriental duck dishes as well, though a spicy Pinot Noir is usually my first choice here. Roast or braised domestic duckling with cherries, bitter orange, or other acidic fruit is best with a fairly substantial red wine, full-flavored but not overly tannic. California Zinfandel is an excellent choice. With the gamier flavors of roast wild duck (mallard, teal, pintail canvasback), I prefer a full-bodied red Burgundy from the Côte de Nuits, such as Chapelle-Chambertin, or a California Pinot Noir. One of the most popular duck dishes is duck breast, roasted until just pink, or sautéed and served with the reduced pan juices. Janet Trefethen of Napa Valley has developed a number of recipes using wild duck, having grown up in wild duck country—the rice fields of the Sacramento delta, where her family has a large farm. Often she marinates slices of duck breast in Trefethen Pinot Noir. Then, when the coals on the outdoor grill are good and hot, John Trefethen grills the meat just to the point of pinkness, while it is still juicy. If it is late enough in autumn, wild mushrooms will garnish the dish, and the Trefethens serve one of their older Pinot Noirs to accompany it. Here, too, Pinot Noir with its fragrant, briary fruit mates well with the flavor of the meat.

Another good choice with duck is Merlot, which is fast becoming one of California's most popular red wines. Merlot has long been used to soften the hardness of young Cabernet Sauvignon, but its soft, round fruit has an appeal all its own. More wineries in California are producing it now, sometimes blended with a bit of Cabernet to give it more backbone. "What I love about Merlot," says Lila Jaeger, one of Napa Valley's creative cooks, "is its versatility. It is not overly heavy, so it goes with a great many things. My husband and I even have it with fish when there are just the two of us because we enjoy a red wine with dinner. If we're having people over, of course, then I usually serve lamb or rabbit."

It is no coincidence that the Jaegers think a lot of Merlot. They produce Inglewood Merlot and are co-owners in Rutherford Hill Winery, which produces one of the best Merlots in California. The Jaegers entertain a great deal and Lila frequently serves rabbit braised with onions and Merlot. This is a most agreeable match. Rabbit is becoming more popular in this country as people discover its appealing flavor. It is often compared to chicken, and looks somewhat like chicken when it is cooked, but it is more flavorful and makes an interesting alternative to chicken or other light meats such as pork or veal.

Merlot is also a compatible choice with lamb. It is a particularly useful choice if you are planning a dinner and must buy young, currently available wines to serve with it. Young Cabernets or Bordeaux, for example, may be too harsh and tannic for immediate enjoyment. California Merlots are ready to drink sooner than Cabernets, for the most part, although the best of them will improve with age, given the chance. They are most appealing at about three to five years of age, however. In addition to Rutherford Hill, other good Merlots are made by Bedell, Bridgehampton, Clos du Bois, Clos du Val, Columbia, Duckhorn, Glen Ellen, Gundlach-Bundschu, Franciscan, Hogue, J. Carey, Robert Keenane, Firestone, Pindar, Plum Creek, Stag's Leap Wine Cellars, Shafer, and Sterling.

Thanksgiving Feast

Our greatest day of celebration in autumn is Thanksgiving. The bounteous Thanksgiving meal poses something of a challenge in selecting wine. Personal preference is, as always, the deciding factor. While the most important thing is to serve the wine you most enjoy drinking, the spiciness of the meal and the variety of flavors that converge on the table at the same time demand that some care be taken in choosing a wine that will be compatible with all of them, or at least most of them. A wine that is too simple may be overwhelmed by such flavorful dishes as mashed turnips, or sweet potatoes topped with marshmallows.

Some people prefer a white wine to go with turkey and there are several that will—including the big, flavorful California Chardonnays and Sauvignon Blancs. In terms of red wine, a Bordeaux or Cabernet Sauvignon that is not too tannic can also be a good choice. Beaujolais *nouveau* is often available in the United States by Thanksgiving. If the vintage was a good one, it can be an excellent selection, likely to please everybody since it is light and fruity and can (and should) be served lightly chilled. Wild turkey, I find, is often not much different from domesticated turkey, but if it does have a gamier flavor, Pinot Noir will go well with it, as will the aforementioned Merlots.

I generally choose a fairly flavorful red wine for Thanksgiving dinner, one that can stand up to some of the pungent "trimmings" that accompany the turkey. Like Gertrude Stein, I cannot make up my mind which dressing I like. Alice B. Toklas wrote in her cookbook that Gertrude could never decide which she liked better—sausage, oyster, or chestnut dressing—so Alice included all three. I usually prepare at least sausage and chestnut. That, plus creamed onions, puréed turnips, homemade cranberry sauce, and several other dishes, makes for a very spicy meal indeed.

My frequent choice for Thanksgiving is Zinfandel—not one of the tannic monsters that do not really go with any food but one of the rounder, more balanced Zinfandels like those of Caymus, Clos du Val, Dry Creek, Ridge Geyserville, Louis M. Martini, Storybook Mountain, Guenoc, Fetzer, Quivira, Preston, or Kendall-Jackson. Another choice is a light chillable red like Gamay Beaujolais or French Beaujolais *nouveau*.

Since Thanksgiving is a particularly American holiday, many people want to serve American wine, and it is a good time to try a local one if you live in a wine-producing area. For Californians, this naturally presents an embarrassment of riches. In other parts of the country, you may be surprised at how appropriate some of the local wines can be. The Pacific Northwest produces some of America's best wine—Merlot, Chardonnay and Sauvignon Blanc from Yakima Valley in Washington, Riesling and Pinot Noir from Oregon and Idaho. Virginia's wineries have swelled to more than forty. If you live in Washington, D.C.—or anywhere in Virginia or Maryland—try a local Merlot or Cabernet Sauvignon, whites like Chardonnay, or proprietary wines like the Countryside White from Oakencroft or Williamsburg's James River White.

More than forty states produce wine, much of it well worth exploring. Here is a partial list of some of the country's best wineries in various states. It is not complete, but it's a start toward getting acquainted with wines grown and made in your own backyard. New vineyards are being planted just about everywhere. One adventurous soul, I hear, is trying to gear up in Alaska.

Arizona: Sonoita, R. W. Webb
Arkansas: Wiederkehr
Colorado: Plum Creek Cellars
Connecticut: Chamard, Crosswoods, Haight, Hopkins
Florida: Lafayette
Georgia: Château Elan, Habersham
Hawaii: Tedeschi
Idaho: Camas, Ste. Chapelle
Illinois: Alto Vineyards, Lynfred
Maine: Bartlett Estate
Maryland: Boordy, Byrd, Catoctin, Montbray
Massachusetts: Chicama (Martha's Vineyard)
Michigan: Boskydel, Château Grand Traverse, Fenn Valley, Good
  Harbor, Madron Lake Hills, Mawby
Minnesota: Alexis Bailly
Mississippi: Claiborne
Missouri: Carver, Hermannhof, Montelle, Mt. Pleasant, Ste.
  Genevieve, Stone Hill
New Jersey: Alba, Tewksbury, Tomasello
New Mexico: Anderson, Blue Teal, La Chiripada, Gruet Brut, Rio
  Valley
New York: Bedell, Benmarl, Bridgehampton, Brotherhood, Cascade
  Mountain, Château Frank, Clinton, Eaton, Glenora, Great
  Western, Hargrave, Knapp, McGregor, Millbrook, North Salem,
  Palmer, Peconic Bay, Pindar, Rivendell, West Park
Ohio: Breitenbach, Brushcreek, Chalet Debonné, Harbor, Markko
Pennsylvania: Allegro, Chaddsford, Naylor, Nissley, York Springs
Rhode Island: Prudence Island, Sakonnet
Tennessee: Laurel Hill
Texas: Domaine Cordier, Fall Creek, Llano Estacado, Messina Hof,
  Pheasant Ridge, Teysha
Virginia: Barboursville, Burnley, Ingelside Plantation, Linden,
  Meredyth, Misty Mountain, Montdomaine, Naked Mountain,
  Oakencroft, Oasis, Piedmont, Prince Michel, Rapidan River,
  Stonewall, Williamsburg
West Virginia: Robert A. Pliska, West-Whitehill
Wisconsin: Wollersheim

The following suggested autumn menus include a variety of meals that celebrate the harvest season in their own particular way, from simple suppers to gustatory spreads like Thanksgiving dinner.

I. HARVEST BARBECUE

Cold Spiced Shrimp and Mussels	MUSCADET

Spit-Roasted Lamb, leg or whole	GIGONDAS
Green Beans à la Nicoise*	
Corn Roasted or Steamed in Shuck	
Cheeses: Tomme de Pyrenées, Bucheron	

Apple Crisp	CALVADOS

MENU NOTES: Muscadet is suggested for the shellfish but other choices would include Mâcon-Villages, Sancerre, Seyval Blanc, Pinot Grigio, Fumé Blanc. Gigondas, the meaty red from the southern Rhône Valley, is excellent with lamb cooked over an open fire. Young, vigorous Cabernet Sauvignon or Merlot would work equally well. Other hearty reds to consider would be Italy's Barbaresco or Brunello di Montalcino, big full-bodied wines that could then continue with the cheese. Calvados, the apple brandy from Normandy, is entirely optional as an after-dinner drink but would be a nice follow-up to the apple crisp.

*See Craig Claiborne's *New York Times Cookbook*.

II. LATE SUMMER/EARLY AUTUMN WEEKEND LUNCH OR SUPPER

Grilled Polenta with Fontina
  Cheese
Sliced Tomatoes with Basil   ORVIETO SECCO
Mixed Greens with
  Vinaigrette
Coarse Bread

MENU NOTES: This meal is simple and satisfying without being heavy, but it depends upon the ripe tomatoes and fresh basil of summer and early fall. Polenta recipes are plentiful these days, in cookbooks like *The Mediterranean Kitchen, The New York Times Cookbook, The New Basics,* and *Marcella Hazan.* Other cheeses, such as Bel Paese or sweet Gorgonzola, may also be used. Young Orvieto, surprisingly, can handle a light vinaigrette very nicely, so don't overdo the salad dressing. The wine should be the youngest available, within a year or so of the vintage at most. A crisp white such as this one is also a good match for mildly savory cheese like Fontina as well as fresh tomato. Fresh berries or other summer fruit can complete the meal.

III. ORIENTAL DINNER

Lettuce-wrapped Spicy
  Chicken
Tangy Stir-fried Beef   BEAUJOLAIS NOUVEAU
Steamed Spinach with   (CHILLED)
  Sesame and Garlic
Chinese Rice

MENU NOTES: Recipes for this menu can be found in Barbara Tropp's wonderful book, *The Modern Art of Chinese Cooking*. While it is suggested for autumn, substitute Beaujolais-Villages or California Gamay Beaujolais if it is past the season for Beaujolais *nouveau*. In either case, the wine should be lightly chilled.

IV. AUTUMN DINNER

Rillettes	SANCERRE ROSÉ
Baked Fish with Fennel **Steamed New Potatoes**	SAVENNIÈRES
Fruit Tarts	BONNY DOON MUSCAT 'VIN DE GLACIÈRE

MENU NOTES: This meal is elegant but simple and quick, especially if you make use of a good local food shop that makes rillettes. To prepare it yourself, check out recipes from Elizabeth David, Madeleine Kamman, or Julia Child. If you also purchase fruit tarts, that leaves only the fish and potatoes to prepare. For Baked Fish with Fennel (from Julie Russo and Sheila Lukins's *The New Basics*) the fish is striped bass, but you can use sea bass, red snapper, turbot, or other meaty fish. Vouvray is a natural for rillettes, but even those labeled *sec* (dry) can be faintly sweet—not a good prelude to the Savennières recommended with the fish. Sancerre Rosé, made entirely from pinot noir, is delightfully fruity but dry and the high acidity is excellent for rillettes. Savennières is one of the Loire's finest dry white wines, with real character and depth that suits fish like bass, snapper, or turbot. The best is Coulée de Serrant.

V. AUTUMN DINNER

Céleri Rémoulade	FUMÉ BLANC
Rabbit Braised in Red Wine Brussels Sprouts	CALIFORNIA MERLOT
Cheese: Bleu d'Auvergne Pears	MUSCAT BEAUMES-DE-VENISE

MENU NOTES: Alternatives to Fumé could include any dry, fresh white wine such as Pinot Grigio or Sauvignon from Italy, or inexpensive California Chardonnays. Rabbit tastes rather like the dark meat of chicken or turkey, so Merlot is a good medium-bodied red wine to go with it. Alternatives would include Gattinara, Chianti Classico, or Rioja. For a keener affinity with the rabbit cooked in wine, use the same red wine in the recipe that you plan to serve at dinner. (Incidentally, rabbit can be found at a good many specialty meat or game shops throughout most of the year.) Bleu d'Auvergne is a savory French blue cheese, firmer and less salty than Roquefort. Paired with fresh ripe pears, it is delicious with the Rhône Valley's noble dessert wine, Muscat Beaumes-de-Venise.

VI. AUTUMN DINNER

Tapenade	EMILIO LUSTAU PALO CORTADO SHERRY
Broiled Whole Red Snapper Potatoes Anna Broccoli with Lemon Butter	MEURSAULT-GENEVRIÈRES
Cheese: Époisses	CORTON
Apricot Tart	CHÂTEAU NAIRAC

MENU NOTES: Palo Cortado is a rich dry sherry, excellent with savory tapenade. Meursault is a white Burgundy, a medium-bodied dry white aged in oak; Genevrières is one of the district's finest vineyards. If you prefer to serve California Chardonnay, look for balanced, elegant styles such as those of Trefethen, Jordan, Iron Horse, Saint Clement, Far Niente, or Simi. Corton is an excellent red Burgundy that would go well with the Burgundian cheese Époisses (other cheese possibilities here would include Reblochon, Chèvre Chabicou or Tome, and Vacherin Mont d'Or). Château Nairac is one of the lighter Sauternes, but any other Sauternes or Barsac, with their overtones of honeyed apricot flavors, would suit the tart.

VII. WEEKEND BRUNCH OR SUPPER

Radishes, Fresh Bread, Sweet Butter	SABLET BLANC OR TAVEL ROSÉ
Saucisson Chaud à la Lyonnaise* **Watercress and Endive Salad**	FLEURIE
Cheeses: Aged Cantal, Cheddar, or Asiago **Seasonal Fruit**	CHÂTEAUNEUF-DU-PAPE*

MENU NOTES: Sablet Blanc is a light Rhône white with enough zip to handle the radishes. Tavel Rosé is fruitier but also up to the

*Patricia Well's *Bistro Cooking.*

job. Fleurie is one of the punchier *cru* Beaujolais; others to consider are Julienás, Morgon, or Moulin-à-Vent. With the full-flavored firm cheeses suggested, any sturdy red wine would work, including Rioja Riserva, Vino Nobile di Montepulciano, Gigondas, California Syrah, or Australian Shiraz. For a casual meal such as this, however, you may want to leave off a bigger wine and simply continue with Beaujolais for the cheese.

VIII. AUTUMN PICNIC

Smoked Salmon
Curried Shrimp
Duck and Green Bean Salad
Cheese and Onion Quiche
Marinated Garden
  Vegetables
Mocha Chocolate Cake

DOMAINE CHANDON BLANC DE NOIRS

MENU NOTES: My first choice for such a portable feast would be pink sparkling wine such as the Domaine Chandon, but there are dozens of others from which to choose, anything from Lembey Brut to Dom Pérignon Rosé. In lieu of sparkling wine, other versatile possibilities would include dry Chenin Blanc, Beaujolais-Villages, Saint-Véran, Italian Chardonnay, blush wines, and dry rosés.

Crudités	**CALIFORNIA BRUT**
Roast Turkey with Sausage and Chestnut Dressing **Sweet Potatoes** **Creamed Onions** **Steamed Kale** **Cranberry—Orange Zest Relish**	**SONOMA ZINFANDEL**
Pumpkin Pie	**LATE-HARVEST GEWÜRZTRAMINER**

MENU NOTES: This all-American feast deserves all-American wines, and you can be as free-ranging as your local wine shops permit. Some excellent Zinfandels to consider from Sonoma County include those of Dry Creek, DeLoach, Foppiano, Preston, Quivira, Ravenswood, Pedroncelli, Ridge Geyserville, and Sebastiani. Though I like Zinfandel at Thanksgiving, there are usually alternatives on my table for those who might prefer something else, sometimes dry Riesling or Fumé Blanc, perhaps a newly arrived Beaujolais *nouveau*, chilled, of course, or Gamay Beaujolais. Late-harvest Gewürztraminer would be particularly complementary to pumpkin pie, but a late-harvest Riesling like Freemark Abbey Edelwein Gold could also be served.

Other Autumn Dishes	**SUGGESTED WINES**
Bourride	**VIN GRIS, DRY ROSÉ**
Braised Lamb with White Beans	**BANDOL ROUGE, SUCH AS DOMAINE TEMPIER**

Bell Peppers Stuffed with Rice and Ground Beef or Lamb	MODERATE-PRICED CABERNET, SUCH AS HAWK CREST
Biryani, Lamb or Chicken	SAINT-EMILION
Choucroute garnie Alsacienne	ALSACE RIESLING, OLDER GEWÜRZTRAMINER (AGE FOUR-FIVE)
Curried Chicken Salad	SAUVIGNON BLANC
Lamb, Roast or Grilled	CABERNET SAUVIGNON, MERLOT, BORDEAUX, CAHORS, BARBARESCO
Grilled Sausages	FLEURIE, JULIÉNAS, BEAUJOLAIS NOUVEAU (LIGHTLY CHILLED)
Grilled Tuna	MERLOT, PINOT NOIR, RIOJA RISERVA, ST. JOSEPH
Roast Veal Shank	VOSNE-ROMANÉE, CLOS DE LA ROCHE, BEAUNE
Stir-fried Beef or Pork in Tangy Sauce	PINOT NOIR, GAMAY BEAUJOLAIS (CHILLED)

ROAST CHICKEN

An amazing variety of wines will go with roast chicken, a popular dish any time of year. The wine may depend very much on the season, what you serve with it, your mood at the moment. In terms of white wines, the choice is narrower, with Chardonnay perhaps first choice; others might include Condrieu, Marsanne (or Marsanne/Roussane), Fiano di Avellino, perhaps Sauvignon Blanc. The diversity of reds for roast chicken are almost endless, to wit:

Bandol rouge	Gigondas
Barbera d'Alba	Margaux
Barbaresco	Mercurey
Beaujolais-Villages	Merlot
Cabernet Sauvignon	Pinot Noir
(medium body and tannins)	Rioja Riserva
Cahors	Rosso di Montalcino
Cairanne (Rhône)	Saint-Emilion
Chianti Riserva	Serradayres
Corbières	Saint-Joseph
Côtes du Lirac	Syrah, Shiraz
Côtes-du-Rhône	Vacqueyras
Cru Beaujolais (Fleurie, Morgon, Julienas, etc.)	Volnay, Santenay
	Zinfandel
Gattinara	

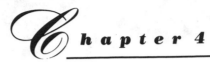

Chapter 4

THE FEASTS
OF WINTER

▼

We were now approaching the Christmas
Festival. . . . It was agreed that all should go to
spend the Night with Colonel Fitzhugh, whose
House is on the Shore of the great River
Potomac. . . . Colonel Fitzhugh showed us the
largest Hospitality. He had Store of good Wine and
other Things to drink, and a Frolic ensued.

THE WILLIAMSBURG ART OF COOKERY, 1742

*A*utumn moves to winter barely skipping a breath or heartbeat. The last bite of pumpkin pie on Thanksgiving weekend puts the cap on autumn, and by Monday we are looking ahead to the year's most concentrated period of celebration and entertaining. The social pace quickens in readiness for Christmas and the turning of the year. People who have not entertained all year play catch-up in December, so to speak.

It is a time of special food and special drink, a time when we pull out all the stops and splurge as hugely as the purse will allow. Caviar and Champagne precede dinners celebrating Hanukkah, Christmas, and the New Year. Roast joints of meat and game appear on the table. Rich fruitcakes, plum puddings, Christmas candy, and other sweets beckon devilishly. Warming winter drinks like mulled wines or the traditional wassail bowl greet those returning from winter outings of caroling, skiing, or skating. The focus of the season is a lavish table of food and drink spilling over with warmth and cheer, around which friends and loved ones gather. Feelings of nostalgia surface, and we turn to ritual and tradition. With all its commercialism and crass "consumeritis" (that is not, perhaps, only a seasonal affliction), Christmas still has the power to work magic in the human heart.

Wine has become the season's signature drink. Statistics show more wine is purchased and consumed during this period than at any other time of year. Most of it is for entertaining, although an increasing amount involves gift-giving. Anyone who appreciates good wine—or wants to learn how to—is pleased to receive a good bottle. Or two. Or a case, if the giver feels generous. The wine we drink most, of course, is sparkling. Be it the genuine article, Champagne from the Champagne region of France, or any one of the dozens of imitators (often excellent) from other regions, Americans are lapping up bubbly as never before.

Were it not the season or occasion for celebrating, serving Champagne would make it seem so. Certainly the most versatile and festive of drinks, it suits a broad range of occasions, from an open house to Christmas brunch to a gala on New Year's Eve. As mentioned earlier, I do not advocate serving Champagne throughout a meal, even on New Year's Eve; however, at parties where finger food is served, or many small portions of different things, it works quite well. In fact, I have learned from experience that for specific types of holiday gatherings Champagne is probably the one drink you can serve throughout. People never seem to tire of it. At a Boxing Day party I once cohosted, for instance, the bar was equipped to handle requests for mixed drinks, white and red wine, or Champagne. The guests all opted for Champagne. It happened, too, at a New Year's Day open house. One might surmise that most people would have overdosed on effervescence by that time.

How does one choose Champagne or other sparkling wine? It comes in a multitude of styles and price ranges today. Is genuine French Champagne really the best? Not necessarily. The "best" of anything as subjective as wine has more to do with personal preference, what tastes best to you. For me, French Champagne has the classic structure, the subtle complexity of aroma and character that I prefer. For some it is too austere. Sparkling wines made elsewhere tend to be fruitier (this does not mean sweeter, although some wines will be), simpler, easier to drink, and certainly easier on the pocketbook. There are many good ones, both domestic and imported, and sometimes their more accessible style suits an occasion better.

Here, perhaps, we should point out the distinction between Champagne with a capital "C" and other sparkling wines. The French have done their best to discourage the use of the generic term *champagne*. Within the Common Market countries it is illegal to use the name for any wine that does not come from the Champagne region in France and is not made by the strict Champagne method *(méthode champenoise)*. The term is not illegal in the United States, but its use must be qualified on the label by geographical appellation, such as California Champagne or New York State Champagne. Many of the newer American producers avoid use of the term altogether and simply label their sparkling wine Brut or Blanc de Noirs.

Champagne

The *méthode champenoise*, which originated in Champagne, is the most expensive and time-consuming process for making sparkling wines, one that evolved over centuries in the Champagne region. The seventeenth-century monk Dom Pérignon, cellarmaster in the Abbey of Hautvillers near Épernay, is usually credited with discovering Champagne. It was indeed a historic moment when he brought his fellow monks running with the cry, "Oh, come quickly, I am drinking stars!" The good monk did not invent the bubbles, however; he merely devised the method for keeping them in the bottle. He discovered that in spring when all of nature begins to awaken from winter's dormancy the wine undergoes a second fermentation. Residual sugar and yeasts that had died down with the onset of cold weather the previous fall were reactivated, releasing carbon dioxide gases that created the bubbles. Back in those days most of the bottles exploded—a disastrous waste of precious substance—but by using heavier bottles that could withstand the pressure and by wiring the cork in place to secure it, Dom Pérignon hit upon the secret for making the world's most celebrated beverage.

Today the process is less primitive and leaves nothing to chance, but it is essentially the same. The still wine is bottled, then a dose of yeast and sugar is added to start a second fermentation. As the yeast converts the sugar to alcohol, carbon dioxide is released and the trapped gas forms the bubbles. The cork is still wired down to hold it in place. Wines that remain longer on the yeasts acquire more character. Most of the better Champagnes, usually vintage Champagne and deluxe cuvées, like Moët's Dom Pérignon, Bollinger Tradition R.D., and Veuve Clicquot La Grande Dame, spend at least three years aging on the yeasts, sometimes four or five, or even longer. Naturally, this extra aging period is costly and it is one of the reasons that these wines are more expensive.

There are three levels of Champagne—vintage, nonvintage, and the deluxe cuvées. Most of the leading Champagne houses make one of the prestige blends such as those named above (a complete list of those available in this country appears on page 85). Special cuvées and vintage Champagnes are usually aged longer than nonvintage and thus have more character. The differences among the various levels, however, are fairly subtle, not readily distinguished unless you taste the wines side by side. If you know and prefer the distinctions, then presumably you are also prepared to pay the extra price for them; otherwise, you will get better value with nonvintage Champagne, which is most representative of the house style.

All Champagne is blended wine, made from white chardonnay grapes and red pinot noir (the juice of the pinot noir grape is clear). Each of the Champagne shippers arrives at a particular blend that characterizes the "house style." The traditional blend is two-thirds pinot noir, which gives body and complexity, and one-third chardonnay, which adds fruit, lightness, and a certain finesse. Champagnes that contain more white grapes, and particularly the blanc de blancs that are made from all chardonnay, taste lighter and fruitier than the more traditional blends of Bollinger, Veuve Clicquot, Krug, or Ayala, which are rich, deep, more complex wines.

Nonvintage remains consistent from year to year by adding up to 20 percent of the blend from previous years, known as *réserve*. Even a vintage Champagne contains a bit of *réserve*. Vintage Champagne carries a certain cachet because vintages are declared only in years when the grapes are exceptional, and not all houses declare vintages the same year. Some, like Pommery et Greno and Moët et Chandon, for instance, made vintage Champagne in 1981. Others made one in 1983, but not in 1981.

If you know what you like in terms of house style—light and

CHAMPAGNE HOUSES AND THEIR BEST CUVÉES

Each of the twenty or so Champagne shippers produces a *tête de cuvée* made from the best lots of grapes and aged longer on the yeasts. Below is a list of Champagne houses and their prestige cuvées.

House	*Label*
Ayala	Blanc de Blancs
Bollinger	Tradition R.D.
	Charles VII
Charbaut	Certificate Blanc de Blancs
Charles Heidsieck	La Royale
Deutz & Geldermann	Cuvée William Deutz
Gosset	Grande Réserve
Heidsieck Monopole	Diamant Bleu
Henriot	Réserve Baron Philippe de Roths-child
Krug	Clos du Mesnil
Laurent-Perrier	Grand Siècle
Louis Roederer	Cristal
Moët et Chandon	Dom Pérignon
	Dom Pérignon Rosé
Mumm	René Lalou
Perrier-Jouët	Fleur de Champagne
	Fleur de Champagne Rosé
Philipponat	Clos des Goisses
Piper-Heidsieck	Florens Louis
Pol Roger	Cuvée Winston Churchill
Ruinart	Dom Ruinart Blanc de Blancs
Salon et Cie	Le Mesnil
Taittinger	Comtes de Champagne Blanc de Blancs
	Comtes de Champagne Rosé
Veuve Clicquot	La Grande Dame

fruity like Perrier-Jouët, for example, or richer and more full-bodied like Krug or Bollinger—then nonvintage is a better buy because it is more consistent. Vintage-dated Champagne, which costs a few dollars more a bottle than nonvintage, will always show a little more of the character of that particular year. Because of the superiority of the grapes, however, vintage Champagne usually lasts longer than nonvintage and even benefits from a few extra years in the bottle, if stored on its side in a quiet, cool place.

The deluxe cuvées, most of which are vintage-dated and therefore made only in superior years, are made from the best lots of grapes in a particular year and aged longer on the yeasts—a costly process. Who can say if they are worth their exalted prices—$50, $75, $100 or more a bottle? Considerable extra attention is lavished on them, however, and they are indeed the wines with the greatest elegance and finesse.

Sparkling wines from elsewhere are improving in quality and increasing in popularity, particularly in California. Since the success of Moët's Domaine Chandon in Napa Valley, other Europeans have come to California to make sparkling wine. Piper-Heidsieck produces Piper-Sonoma, Pommery owns a chunk of Sharffenberger, Mumm has Domaine Mumm, and Taittinger has Domaine Carneros. Other illustrious Champagne houses are represented as well in Roederer Estate and Maison Deutz. The Spanish firm of Freixenet built Gloria Ferrer Carneros, and Codorníu Napa is also in Carneros.

Other leading names in California sparkling wine are Schramsberg, Jordan, Korbel (the oldest), Iron Horse, Mirassou, Hanns Kornell, Chateau Saint Jean, Glen Ellen, Beaulieu, Culbertson, Van der Kamp, Shadow Creek, S. Anderson, and Wente, all of whom employ the *méthode champenoise* used in making French Champagne and say so on the bottle.

California sparkling wines have forced us to become familiar with new terms that characterize the various styles of wine. Here are some of those most commonly used:

BRUT This is the driest of French Champagne, although some Bruts seem to be drier than others. In California the term is used for dry sparkling wine, usually blended from both pinot noir and chardonnay grapes, and perhaps pinot blanc. Among all sparkling wines, including Champagne, the dryness of Brut varies somewhat, ranging from bone-dry to just off-dry, but here again, taste preference determines choice.

BLANC DE BLANCS This term is used for wines made from all white grapes. Chardonnay (and only chardonnay in top French Champagne) is the most common choice, although other varieties are sometimes used. Chenin blanc is used in the Loire Valley and occasionally in California. Local white varieties are used in Spain.

BLANC DE NOIR(S) This term refers to white wine made from black (or red) grapes, specifically pinot noir. Colors vary a bit in these wines, depending on how they are made. Color pigments in the grape skins may be extracted, intentionally or unintentionally. Some blanc de noirs are pale gold, others range from slightly pink to vividly pink.

TÊTE DE CUVÉE This French term, meaning "top blend," signifies the winery's best (or at least its most expensive) sparkling wine.

NATURAL, AU NATURAL Drier than Brut, this term is used by wineries whose Brut is not bone-dry.

Other Sparkling Wines

Some very attractive sparkling wines are made in the Loire Valley in France. According to French law, no wine made outside the Champagne region may be called Champagne, so others are known as *vins mousseux* (sparkling wines). Names to look for are Bouvet Brut, Monmousseau, and Gratien & Meyer Brut, both made from chenin blanc near the Loire towns of Saumur and Vouvray.

Brut spumante is Italian for "dry sparkling," and must not be confused with Asti *spumante*, the sweet sparkling Muscat from the Piedmont region. Some Italian producers, such as Ferrari and Contratto, use the *méthode champenoise* for making Brut *spumante*, but good ones are also made using simpler methods by such firms as Gancia, Cavit, and Bolla. Some of the best values in *méthode champenoise* wines are from Spain, specifically Cordorníu Gran Brut, Friexenet Cordon Negro, and Lembey Brut Premiere.

One can make excellent use of these less expensive wines in Champagne punches or mixed drinks. I recall one Christmas when I had an open house and did not know how many guests would attend. After poring over a number of books with drink recipes, I finally just devised one of my own that would work no matter how many showed up. I started with a pint of hulled fresh strawberries and one package of frozen peaches, which went into the blender long enough to whip them into a peach gold froth. Half a dozen bottles of Korbel Brut were chilling in the refrigerator, along with extra quantities of fruit in case the number of guests swelled beyond my estimate. It did, but I was ready. As more friends appeared it was simple to pour out an ounce or so of the fruit mixture, whipping up more as needed, and top it off with two or three ounces of bubbly. The most frequent response was "Fabulous!" (Recipes for this and other holiday drinks and punches will be found in Chapter 6.)

One of the best ways to discover which Champagne or sparkling wine you prefer is to give a tasting. Invite a dozen people, ask each to bring a different bottle, and taste the wines blind (bottles wrapped so no one is influenced by the labels). Starting on page 210 there is advice on how to plan such a tasting.

Winter's Sturdy Reds

The wines of winter are also the hearty reds—big, rich Burgundies like Chambertin, Richebourg, and Corton; Rhônes like Hermitage, Côte Rôtie, and occasionally Châteauneuf-du-Pape; dark Barolos and Barbarescos from the Italian Piedmont; and California's weightier Cabernets, Zinfandels, and Rhone blends. They are fine with winter foods like joints of roast meat, game, robust stews, and meaty casseroles.

Game is a splendid specialty of the winter season. When I was growing up we had our annual turkey on Thanksgiving. At the family feast on Christmas Eve, however, we dined on game, usually wildfowl from the flocks of wild duck and geese that streamed down the Mississippi flyway during December on their way to winter feeding grounds on the Gulf Coast. If the hunter's eye was keen, and it usuallly was, we feasted on the rich, dark meat of mallards, pintails, or, when the game limit permitted, a brace of blue geese or succulent Canadas.

The voluminous red Burgundies of the Côte d'Or are the classic accompaniment to game. Burgundy's famed "golden slopes" yield wines of grandeur like Chambertin, Musigny, Clos Vougeot, Richebourg, and La Tâche that are excellent with venison cloaked in a dark wine sauce. Lighter Burgundies, such as Nuits-Saint-Georges, Pommard, Beaune, and Volnay, are superb with lighter game such as pheasant and wild duck.

The character of a good Burgundy, even those from well-ripened vintages like 1978, is full and heady, but not really heavy. Plumpness of flavor and opulent aroma—I have had Burgundies that filled a whole room with their fragrance—make them among the most alluring of red wines. Unfortunately, many Burgundies have soared out of reach in terms of price. Current vintages of La Tâche, for instance, are well over $200 a bottle; the price ranges from $35 to $100 or more for other top ones. I well remember the days when I passed over simple Pommard at $5 or $8 a bottle and splurged $10 or $12 on Richebourg and La Tâche. Today those "simple" bottles are $40 or more—Pommard's Revenge!

New World Pinot Noirs

California has made tremendous strides with Burgundy's red grape, pinot noir, in the last several years. After decades of striving and experimenting with the grape, some lovely (and lively) Pinot Noirs have emerged, rich in flavor and texture and excellent with a variety of foods. Oregon also produces elegant and appealing Pinots, great ones when vintage conditions are just right. The Oregon climate is cool and the growing season long, similar in those respects to Burgundy. Similar also, unfortunately, is the threat of rain during harvest. Oregon Pinot Noirs are lighter than most from California but not necessarily less intense in good vintages, especially the Reserve Pinots. Some of the best producers of Pinot Noir are:

California	Oregon
Acacia	Adelsheim Ponzi
Au Bon Climat	Amity
Beaulieu Carneros	Bethel Heights
Calera	Cameron
Carneros Creek	Elk Cove
Chalone	The Eyrie Vineyard
David Bruce	Hidden Springs
Davis Bynum	Knudsen-Erath
Dehlinger	Oak Knoll
Gary Farrell	Ponzi
Iron Horse	Rex Hill
Robert Mondavi	Sokol-Blosser
Robert Stemmler	Tualatin
Saintsbury	
Sinskey	
Sterling Winery Lake	
Wild Horse Winery	
Williams-Selyem	

Robust reds from the Rhône Valley are also good choices for game dishes, especially the richer ones like venison or wild hare or boar. The noble grape syrah is used for Hermitage and Côte Rôtie, the two best reds from the Rhône. Well-aged Hermitage has a flinty richness about it that can stop conversation at a dinner table—and has done so more than once at mine. Hermitage can live a very long time if stored properly, as attested to by George Saintsbury in *Notes on a Cellar Book*. Saintsbury was the earliest chronicler of wine-tasting notes, which he began keeping when he started laying down a cellar in England in the late nineteenth century.

At a local wine merchant in London, Saintsbury had acquired

an 1846 Hermitage, which he drank when the wine was forty years old. "Now most red wines," he wrote, "are either past their best, or have no best to come to, at that age. . . . But my Hermitage showed not the slightest mark or presage of enfeeblement . . . it was the *manliest* wine I ever drank; and age had softened and polished all that might have been rough in its youth."

Hermitage does not have to be forty years old to be enjoyed, although cellaring one from a good vintage, like 1985 or 1988, might well bring similar rewards, and far sooner. I enjoy a good Hermitage or Côte Rôtie with a full-flavored cheese, a savory Cheddar or Parmesan. In fact, many of the big red wines can be excellent for the cheese course in a wine dinner, as noted in Chapter 1.

Somewhat less magisterial are the lighter Rhône reds, although they are still quite sturdy—Gigondas, Vacqueyras, Châteauneuf-du-Pape. These wines, as well as many of the pleasantly rugged Italian reds like Barbera and Dolcetto, Carmignano, and Rubesco, work well with the thick soups, stews, and casseroles of late winter.

This is also an opportunity to try some of the California reds made from Rhône varietals like Syrah, Mourvèdre, Grenache, and Cinsaut. California's Rhône specialists, dubbed the "Rhône Rangers," are a growing bunch that includes Bonny Doon, Qupé, Cline Cellars, Joseph Phelps, McDowell, Edmunds St. John, and Jade Mountain, among others. They produce stylish and sometimes quite exciting reds from single varieties like syrah or mourvèdre, or robust blends of two or more grapes. Bonny Doon Le Cigare Volant, for example, is a blend of syrah, grenache, and mourvèdre in more or less equal proportions. The quirky name means "the flying cigar" and refers to a UFO sighting in the Rhône Valley in 1954; the full story is told on the label. Various other Rhône blends worth exploring are Cline Oakley Cuvée, Edmunds St. John Les Côtes Sauvage, McDowell Le Tresor, Santino Satyricon.

Several California wineries are also working with white grapes from the Rhône, Marsanne, Roussanne (Bonny Doon, Qupé), and Viognier (Bonny Doon, Calera, Joseph Phelps, La Jota, Ritchie Creek, and Sierra Vista). Some of these wines are quite extraordinary, such as Bonny Doon Le Sophiste, Qupé Marsanne, and the Viogniers of Calera, La Jota, and Ritchie Creek. Very small quantities of Rhône varietals or blends are produced, but new vineyards are steadily being planted to remedy that.

Once the holidays are over life calms down a bit, but in many parts of the country a long stretch of winter cold sets in. This is a time of year I always welcome. How divine it is to burrow in and hibernate for a spell, dive into a pile of neglected work, or a good book, or just putter around the kitchen cooking up simple, nourishing foods—rib-sticking soups, for instance. "Beautiful soup!" crooned the Mock Turtle in *Alice in Wonderland*. "Who cares for fish, Game or any other dish. . . . Soup of the evening, beautiful, beautiful soup." Surely he meant substantial potages like French onion, lentil, and sausage, split pea with ham, or thick clam chowder. Except with the chowder, I would take a red wine with soups of texture; any of the light Rhônes mentioned earlier would go well, or consider some of the California generic wines like Fetzer Premium Red or Trefethen's Eshcol. With chowder, if I have any wine at all, it is usually something quite simple, an inexpensive imported *vin de table* or a dry California table wine like Eshcol White or Pinot Blanc.

White wines are as much in evidence in winter as any other time of year, with light meats such as chicken, turkey, or veal and with fish and shellfish. During the winter months oysters are at their most delectable. "Cicero ate oysters to nourish his eloquence," wrote M. F. K. Fisher. But did he wash them down with a good Chablis? Not in the first century B.C. Oysters and Chablis are one of those classic combinations that work supremely well. A good French Chablis is what is meant here, not the ordinary blended white of that name from California, which has none of the dry, crisp, flinty edge of true Chablis.

The Chablis region in northern Burgundy has soil full of calcium that gives the wine a wondrous link with mineral-rich oysters and other shellfish. There are other dry whites to drink with oysters, namely Muscadet, the sprightly white made in the western Loire Valley near the Atlantic, with its rich coastal oysterbeds. Champagne is a popular match for oysters. Chardonnay and Sancerre or California Sauvignon Blancs also make excellent partners. So does a good beer. But I will always take Chablis if I can get it.

The menus suggested for winter meals are rather hearty, you will note. Roast goose makes a lovely Christmas dinner but is delicious throughout the months that it is available. *Ossobuco*, Milan-style braised veal shanks, is a favorite of mine, as is *risotto*, the unique Italian rice dish commonly served with it. Cassoulet, the hearty bean-and-meat stew of the Midi region in France, is solidly satisfying fare that soothes and comforts against the chilly blasts of late winter, although by this time brief breaks in the weather already hint of the season ahead: "O Wind, if Winter comes, can Spring be far behind?"

WINTER MENUS

I. HOLIDAY DINNER

Oysters	CHABLIS GRAND CRU
Roast Goose	CALIFORNIA PINOT NOIR
Wild Rice with Chestnuts	NUITS-SAINT-GEORGES
Braised Fennel	
Christmas Fruitcake	COCKBURN'S RESERVE PORT

MENU NOTES: Alternates to the classic match of oysters and Chablis are Muscadet, Washington Semillon, and Champagne. Acacia makes excellent Pinot Noir, but there are other good ones to consider, such as those of Robert Mondavi, Calera, David Bruce, Knudsen-Erath, Trefethen (see list on page 90). Red Burgundies such as Nuits-Saint-Georges, Corton, Clos des Mouches, or Pommard are also fine selections for this menu. The port can be vintage-character ruby like the Cockburn or a mellow tawny like Warre's Nimrod; either would complement the rich sweetness of holiday fruitcake.

Roast Red Peppers with Fresh Mozzarella	TOSCANO BIANCO
Ossobuco Milanese*	GATTINARA, BARBARESCO
Risotto	(AGED EIGHT TO TEN YEARS)
Spinach Salad	
Cheese: Parmigiano- Reggiano	**1978** BAROLO
Macedoine of Fruits	GRAPPA

MENU NOTES: Mature Gattinara, Barbaresco, or Chianti Riserva is suggested with Ossobuco. Polenta or pasta can substitute for Risotto. The 1978 Barolos are magnificent wines, although scarce; they are best set off by a fine cheese like aged Parmesan; look for a 1982 Barolo if you cannot find a 1978. Grappa is an intense grape brandy from Italy, a fiery eau-de-vie that should be experienced at least once.

*See Craig Claiborne, Marcella Hazan, or Julie Rosso and Sheila Lukins's *The New Basics*.

Niçoise Olives and Celery Hearts	PINOT BLANC
Cassoulet Toulousaine*	CAHORS
Red and Green Pepper Salad	
Garlic Bread	

Cheese: Doux de Montagne	CÔTE RÔTIE

Fruit Tarts	ARMAGNAC

MENU NOTES: This hearty buffet starts off simply with tiny piquant black olives and crisp celery sticks, accompanied by a dry Pinot Blanc from Alsace or California. Cahors is a medium-bodied red from southwestern France; equally suitable, however, would be one of the meatier Beaujolais such as Morgon or Moulin-à-Vent, or one of the fruity Midi reds from Corbières or Rousillon. Doux de Montagne is a semifirm cheese from the Pyrenees, but any rustic cheese could be substituted and would suit a lusty, red-blooded wine like Côte Rôtie from the Rhone or even a Gigondas. Armagnac is the heartwarming brandy of Gascony and a good digestif after a meal such as this one (except for designated drivers!)

*Paula Wolfert's *The Cooking of Southwest France*

Winter Fruit Compote	**MIMOSAS**
Pipérade	
Sausage Cakes	

Toasted Baguettes	**COFFEE AND TEA**

MENU NOTES: Mimosas, made with orange juice and sparkling wine, are a delightful way to toast Christmas. (The recipe for the drink appears on page 161.) *Pipérade* is a flavorful Basque-country omelet made with green peppers, tomatoes, and onions; it also makes an excellent luncheon or supper dish and goes well with a light red wine such as Côtes du Ventoux.

V. APRÈS-SKI SUPPER

	MULLED WINE

Lentil and Sausage Soup	**BARBERA D'ALBA**
Pissaladière*	
Green Salad	
Green Apple Sauce	
Almond Cookies	

MENU NOTES: This meal is intended as simple but savory nourishment after strenuous outdoor activity. It sounds like a lot, but if served in reasonable portions—a cup of mulled wine as a warm-up, a bowl of soup, a slice of *pissaladière* (Provençal onion tart), a fresh green salad, and homemade applesauce—it need not be heavy unless you are overgenerous (ill-advised in any case after vigorous exercise). The recipe for mulled wine appears on pages 169–70.

*See Julie Rosso and Sheila Lukins's *The Silver Palate Cookbook*.

Other Winter Dishes	Suggested Wines
Cassoulet	Cahors, Corbières, Madiran, California Syrah or Rhône blends (Le Cigare Volant)
Beef Stew, such as *daube* or *carbonnade*	Châteauneuf-du-Pape, Vino Nobile di Montepulciano, Pesquera, Gran Coronas, Dão
Breast of Pheasant	Reserve Pinot Noir, Clos de la Roche, Beaune Clos des Mouches
Coq au Vin	Mercurey, Vacqueyras, Chinon, Merlot, or Pomerol
French Onion Soup	Mâcon-Blanc, or a light red such as Côtes du Ventoux (lightly chilled)
Fresh Oysters	Chablis, *grand* or *premier cru* Muscadet, Champagne, Sémillon
Ossobuco	Gattinara, Carmignano, Chianti Riserva, Cabernet, or Merlot
Pork Loin with Prunes	Bandol Rouge, Dolcetto d'Alba, Zinfandel
Risotto with Mushrooms or Truffles	Oaky Chardonnay, such as Gaja, Jermann, Robert Mondavi Reserve
Roast Beef	Bordeaux, Cabernet Sauvignon Hermitage
Roast Duck or Goose	Red Burgundy, Pinot Noir, Shiraz, Riesling *Spätlese*
Venison (stew or with rich sauce)	Barolo, Hermitage, Côte Rotie, Cornas, Shiraz, Mourvédre, Syrah, Zinfandel, Petite Syrah, Rhone blends such as Orion, Les Cotes Sauvages
Venison Steak, rare	Red Burgundy

Chapter 5

WELCOMING SPRING'S FRESH FLAVORS

▼

And everywhere, in every village or great temple of gastronomy, there were the proper wines, whether they came out of a spigot into a thick tumbler or slipped from a cradled cobwebbed bottle into the bottoms of glasses that rang thinly in the faintest stir of air.

M. F. K. FISHER, *The Gastronomical Me*

When winter snows have vanished and the chilly winds of March have softened, spring arrives to usher in new foods—seasonal fish like salmon, shad, and, later, soft-shell crabs, lighter meats like baby spring lamb, capon, pork, and veal. There is a renewed emphasis on white wines and lighter red wines, and one's mood is more than ready for the change. Just as I yearn for robust reds in autumn, in the spring I look forward to the arrival of fresh, youthful white wines from the previous vintage.

The cycle of the vine, and of winemaking, follows the rhythms of nature so tangibly that one can easily track it. A vineyard can seem a fairly desolate place near the end of winter, when the vines have been pruned and tied to their training wires. They stand naked in neat rows, looking cold and forlorn and very vulnerable. In fact, they are not: at this stage they are well protected by the tough kernel that encloses the buds. Soon, however, as the days lengthen and the sun tilts higher to warm the earth, the vines begin responding to nature's pull and tug. At the same moment that the early spring jonquils and crocuses appear, the season of growth begins anew in the vineyard as well.

The young wines that start to appear in spring—whites of the Loire Valley like Muscadet and Vouvray, Mâcon-Villages, Beaujolais, California Rieslings, Fumé Blanc, Chenin Blanc, Gewürztraminer, even a few Chardonnays—have a fruity charm that lends itself well to occasions for spring entertaining, particularly at lunch or weekend brunches.

One dish I particularly delight in is the Italian specialty pasta primavera, pasta with spring vegetables. This dish has become so popular that menus now list it year-round. Originally, however, the name signified a genuine spring dish, garnished with the tiny new vegetables of the season. The best one I ever had was in California, at a wonderful old hotel restaurant called the New Boonville Hotel, since abandoned, then revived. It still looked like a relic when I was there, slightly seedy and run-down on the outside, although inside the kitchen and dining rooms had been refurbished in simple, no-nonsense neatness. The visual delight of the place was its garden, marvelously landscaped, meticulously tended, and glorious to look at with its profusion of flowers, herbs, and vegetables.

After a stroll through the garden, our table was ready, and, as I quite often do, I ordered pasta primavera, which my friend and I were to share as a first course. What a surprise when it arrived, festooned with tiny carrots, peas, pearl onions, and various infant legumes plucked from the garden a short time before. We were glad we had ordered a light-bodied Chardonnay that did not overwhelm the subtle flavors of such a delicate dish. Italy, of course, has a number of soft, dry white wines that are perfect with the lighter pasta dishes. Pinot Bianco from the northestern regions of Trentino and Friuli is an excellent choice. So is Chardonnay from the same cool regions, or Pinot Grigio, although I find the latter better with certain seafood pasta dishes. Soave is always an agreeable match, but it is such a cliché now that I find myself looking for one of the other whites that have more character.

Pastas with cream sauces, such as fettucine Alfredo, call for white wine with a little more body, such as Gavi. Gavi used to be something of a rarity in the United States, but as Americans have become more familiar with the better Italian wines, it is more widely available, especially on restaurant wine lists. Dry and quite crisp, it is fuller in flavor and a bit weightier than other northern Italian whites, making it a good choice for many fish and chicken dishes.

The world of pasta has astonishing variety, as Americans continue to discover, either traveling through Italy or dining at the increasing number of fine Italian restaurants here. On one of my trips through Italy, I decided to allow myself pasta at every meal until I grew tired of it. To my amazement, in the entire three weeks I never did. Why I should have found that so surprising I cannot imagine—Italians have it practically every day of the year, sometimes twice a day.

Whenever possible, or appropriate, I like to match up wines and foods that would typically accompany one another in the country where they originated. I do not make a fetish of it, however, particularly when I am serving pasta at home or ordering it in restaurants that are not exclusively Italian. Fortunately, so many good Italian wines are available now that one need not rely solely on old dependables like Chianti, Soave, or Corvo. When it comes to pasta, the old rules of white with fish and red with meat become a bit blurred. I can usually drink a dry white wine with a meat-sauce pasta such as *al ragú* (Bolognese style) as easily as I can a red wine. Very often I prefer a light red to go with pasta and shellfish, particularly if it is made with a rich, spicy tomato sauce. Chianti is too acidic for shellfish, but one of the light Cabernet Sauvignons or Merlots from the Veneto or Friuli would be fine. The heartier pastas like *carbonara, putanesca,* or *amatriciana,* all of which have rich, pungent flavor, can take meatier reds like Barbera, Rosso di Montalcino, Dolcetto, and certainly Chianti. Valtellina reds like Grumello or Sassella are other wines to consider as well.

Pasta Chart

Ubiquitous pasta! We love it, in all its endless variations. It's not the pasta we consider when choosing wine, however; it's what goes on it (or in it) that determines what the wine should be. Pasta is not especially seasonal unless the topping (white truffles, for instance) is, but some pastas do seem to have a certain proclivity for spring, say, or winter. The list below suggests matches for some of the most popular and frequently encountered pastas. Some pastas, you will note, are compatible with a remarkable variety of wines.

Spring	Wine
Pasta Primavera	Vernaccia di San Gimignano, Orvieto, Gavi
	Dry Riesling from Alsace, California, New York, or Washington (such as Hogue's Schwartzman Vineyard)
	Pinot Blanc from Alsace, Italy, or California
	Bourgogne Aligoté
	Dry Chenin Blanc (Preston, Girard, Hacienda)
Pasta with cream sauce (Alfredo, others)	Italian Chardonnay from Trentino, Alto-Adige, Tre Venezie, Arneis, Gavi, Soave Classico

Summer

Pasta with Seafood: Crab Lobster, Shrimp	Chardonnay, white Burgundy such as Rully, Montagny, Chablis, Meursault
Mussels, Scallops, Clams	Pinot Grigio, Muscadet
Salmon, Tuna	Sauvignon Blanc, including Sancerre or light red such as Oregon Pinot Noir, Sancerre Rouge; also *vin gris*
Pasta Mediterranean Style (tomatoes, garlic, herbs)	Crisp, somewhat austere white such as Pinot Grigio, Sablet Blanc (Rhône), Chilean Sauvignon Blanc; dry rosés from Provence
Pasta with Pesto	Pinot Grigio, especially riper styles like Livio Felluga

Canelloni	Chardonnay from Trentino, Tre Venezie, Soave Classico, Pomino Bianco (Frescobaldi), Coltibuono Bianco, Orvieto *secco*, Ruffino Libaio

Fall:

Pasta with Wild Mushrooms	Oaky Chardonnay, if you want white wine; Meursault, Chassagne-Montrachet. Red: Burgundy, Chianti Riserva
Pasta with White Truffles	Barbaresco (five to ten years old); white Burgundy or full-bodied Italian Chardonnay, such as Gaja, Pio Cesare, or Ca' del Bosco
Pasta Puttanesca	Lachryma Christi Rosso, Rosso di Montalcino, Montepulciano d'Abruzzi Greco di Tufo

Winter:

Ravioli, Fusilli, Tubes, etc., with Meat Sauce	Chianti Riserva, Carmignano, Barbera d'Alba, Rubesco
Carbonara	Rosso di Montalcino, Barbera, Chianti Classico, Gattinara, dry rosé
Duck Sausage	Dolcetto d'Alba, Pinot Nero, Montepulciano d'Abruzzo
Lasagna	Grumello, Barbera, Chianti Riserva, Ghemme

Admittedly it is somewhat arbitrary to treat fish in this season since we have it year-round. Still, after the heavier dishes of winter, fish dishes leap to mind rather quickly. Many species of fish do make a special appearance in spring. The silver salmon begins its first mysterious leap homeward to spawn. The bluefish starts its run up the Atlantic coast. Louisiana redfish scurry out of the bayous and into the open waters of the Gulf; blue crabs scuttle into spawning grounds in the marshes of the Chesapeake Bay. Inland, the bass are biting once again, and speckled trout entice eager fishermen to flyfishing waters.

If you think only white wine with fish, think again when it comes to salmon. I adore salmon, all types—Chinook, coho, sockeye, or the more delicately flavored Atlantic species. It is easy to prepare and difficult to ruin except by overcooking, but it does pose a challenge when selecting a wine to go with it. Red-fleshed salmon, such as sockeye, has the highest oil content and most pronounced flavor. Pink-fleshed salmon, such as coho (also known as silver) is more delicate but still oilier than most fish. For this reason a light red wine can be an excellent choice, something like Beaujolais-Villages (best if lightly chilled) or a mature red Burgundy from the Côte de Beaune, like Volnay or Pommard. Lighter Cabernets can also be suitable, but not if they are too young or too tannic, setting up a bitter taste in both the wine and the fish.

The choice of wine also depends upon how the fish is prepared— it can be poached, broiled, marinated, grilled, pan-fried, and sauced in myriad ways. The most spectacular method I ever witnessed takes place every summer at Oregon's Pinot Noir festival in McMinnville—the traditional method used by local Indians a century ago. Huge fillets of freshly caught chinook are skewered on green saplings and grilled over an open alder-log fire. Alder burns very hot, sealing in the juices that keep the fish moist and succulent. Diners have the choice of Oregon Pinot Noir, Pinot Gris, or Chardonnay, but I invariably settle on Pinot Noir, which suits the slightly smoked flavor of the salmon. Others, however, prefer the Pinot Gris or Chardonnay. If you choose white, however, remember that acidity is paramount. Pinot Gris is tartly crisp and fruity, a particularly good match for poached salmon with dill sauce.

I once had an attractive, well-balanced Zinfandel with red salmon at a California luncheon, but the combination did not work well. Zinfandel is too assertively fruity for fish, in my view, although Zinfandel made in a *nouveau* style and therefore served lightly chilled might work in some cases. The sauce served with salmon can make a big difference in whether to choose red or white wine. Poached pink salmon in *beurre blanc* with white wine will be better with a full-bodied white wine, either a full-flavored white Burgundy like Corton-Charlemagne or Montrachet or one of the oakier California Chardonnays, such as those of Robert Mondavi, Grgich Hills, Sanford, Chateau Woltner, Matanzas Creek, Morgan, or Château Saint Jean Robert Young Vineyard. Like white Burgundies, Chardonnays aged in oak have a richness and dimension that complement the fish and its sauce.

Bluefish, like mackerel, is another rather oily species that is often better served by a light red wine than having it overpower a white. I like to cook bluefish by baking it whole, stuffed with herbs, slivered almonds, black currants, and bread crumbs. Very few white wines work with bluefish, and I've tried many. I find that oak-aged Sauvignon Blancs from wineries like Sterling, Stag's Leap, Cakebread, Silverado, and Mondavi are often able to handle bluefish very well indeed. Most recently, however, I have taken to serving chilled Côte de Brouilly, the lightest of the village Beaujolais, with blues, and it seems to work better than anything else.

Sauce Is Key

As mentioned earlier, the sauce involved—or the absence of sauce—largely determines the type of wine you choose to go with fish, as is true with any sort of dish. Simple broiled or sautéed fish, particularly delicately flavored ones such as trout, sole, or various members of the perch family, require a delicate white—I think first of dry Riesling, or just off-dry but light Chardonnays such as Mâcon-Villages or Saint-Véran, the Italian Lugana or Pinot Bianco. Dry Chenin Blancs can work well, too; sweet ones less well, I think. By contrast, a light Mosel Riesling, even if it is lightly sweet, is often delicious with simple fish dishes because of its higher acidity. Dry Alsace Rieslings can be quite lovely and best at three or four years old when they are no longer austere. Richer Rieslings from Alsace, those labeled Réserve Personnel or Exceptionnel, are too strong and go better with fish in classic sauces such as *beurre blanc* or *cardinal*.

Classically sauced fish (if you will forgive the pun) are best with classic white wines—white Graves from Bordeaux, white Burgundy, specifically anything from the Puligny-Montrachet level upward, and the more elegant and complex California Chardonnays. These dishes include filet of striped bass, poached turbot, stuffed filet of sole in white wine sauce, baked red snapper, and the like. Again, it is a good idea to use in cooking a bit of the wine you will be drinking if the recipe calls for wine. The connection is subtle, but a delight to the discerning palate.

Shellfish and Crustacea

Once, during a visit to the Cognac region of France, several of us made an excursion to the port of La Rochelle, ancient stronghold of the Huguenots and embarkation point for the noble amber spirit the Dutch christened *brandewijn*, "burnt wine," or brandy. La Rochelle has a wonderful old harbor, still active, although mainly as a fishing port and thus spared the dreadful modernization that has taken over more international shipping centers. The same implacable stone towers that stood as bastions in the 1700s, when Cognac was a center for the salt trade instead of brandy, guard its exit to the open sea.

La Rochelle's cobblestoned quai is lined with marine shops, restaurants, and fishmongers, interspersed with gift shops full of cheap bric-a-brac to lure tourists. But oh, what a wild array of seafood! Wooden bins in front of restaurants and fish stalls display the day's catch, spilling over with *fruits de mer* of every hue and shape—langoustes of glistening pink opalescence, delicate bone-colored cockles, mossy green oysters with jagged shells that look like pieces hacked off the ocean's rocky edge, and shiny black mussels with scruffy beards. Whole fish, eyes fixed in bright beady stare, lie stacked in neatly scalloped layers of pink and silver. The clean, brisk tang of ocean freshness permeates the air, and the display does its work well, whetting the appetite, setting the mouth awater.

Our destination for dinner that evening was the nearby coastal town of Marennes, famed for its oyster beds. When we finally arrived, ravenous and thirsty, chilled bottles of the local white wine, Gros Plant du Pays Nantais, awaited us. The restaurant, called Claires (named for the local oyster), is well known in those parts for its seafood specialties. Within minutes of our arrival great straw platters piled high with shellfish were set before us—marinated mussels, langoustes, shrimp, and, best of all, the local marsh-cultivated oyster, more delicate than those fished straight from the sea because they are nourished on the slightly less briny marsh waters. We washed them down with a crisp, bone-dry Gros Plant, marveling at how perfectly its brisk acidic edge complemented the shellfish.

Gros Plant is rarely available in the United States. It is one of those mild white wines that is charmingly fresh on the spot but overstabilized for travel and never as good far from home, much less across an ocean. Still, it is well worth trying when you are anywhere in Brittany or the western end of the Loire. The better wine of the region is Muscadet, which we do get here in reasonable quantity. Good Muscadet is excellent with raw oysters and is the wine I turn to if I cannot have a good French Chablis, which is my first choice with oysters. Muscadet is a simple wine and best when it is quite young and fresh, within a year or so of the vintage. Anything older lacks freshness and fruit, without which the wine is sharp and acid.

Muscadet also can be a good choice with shad roe, usually fairly delicate if prepared well. Likewise the combination is appropriate with versions that include the mother fish with its very tender and sweet flesh. Muscadet is a little severe, however, for that other springtime specialty, soft-shell crabs. These succulent creatures, usually broiled or sautéed in simple fashion, are better with a slightly fuller white like Saint-Véran or Pouilly-Fruissé. Another good choice here would be the Loire Valley white wine Pouilly-Fumé; its citruslike Sauvignon Blanc character has the needed acidity but is fuller and rounder than Muscadet.

Red wine with shellfish? Why not? ask the Bordelais. One of the regional specialties in Bordeaux, which is forty miles or so inland from oyster breeding grounds in Arcachon, is a platter of raw oysters accompanied by tiny spicy grilled sausages, an appetizer traditionally served with a light red Bordeaux. The combination sounds bizarre and it tastes a bit that way, too, but it does work. The red wine has to be a light one, not tannic or astringent, and it is best if served at ideal cellar temperature, about 55 to 60 degrees.

Bouillabaisse

This Mediterranean extravaganza, with its pungently flavored broth and potpourri of herby aromas, will overpower most wines—as anyone knows who has ever bent over a steaming bowl of it. Do not choose anything complex, which would be lost among the saffron and spices. Bouillabaisse is best with a relatively simple white or rosé, but one with some backbone such as Crozes-Hermitage Blanc or Tavel Rosé. Some people prefer a simple, unassuming red with bouillabaisse, such as Côtes du Rhône. A lightly cooled Côtes-de-Provence dry rosé is often served with the dish along the Côte d'Azur.

Spring Meats

Early spring in many parts of the country can be as frigid as the dead of winter, certainly snowier on occasion, a boon for spring skiers and reason enough not to abandon heartier foods and wines too soon. Meat stews and roasts, cassoulet, and thick soups are the best hedge against March's bluster. They afford perhaps the last opportunity to serve robust reds until fall and I always like to work in a good hefty Barolo, Côte Rôtie, or Syrah, perhaps even an Amarone that never made it to table during the earlier winter season. If my main course is not hearty enough, then I will choose such a wine for the cheese course, making sure that the cheese is one with plenty of savory character. We have many more choices of good cheeses than we used to, rather special ones like Caciotta, aged Asiago or Gouda, Livarot, genuine Muenster from Alsace, or various blues—any of which calls for a fine full-blooded red. And we now have hearty American cheeses, too—aged Gouda and Dry Jack, Cheddar, Cacciota, and a great diversity of goat cheese.

As I have mentioned, the lighter meats we often turn to in spring are spring lamb, pork, fowl, and veal. When Henri IV advocated a chicken in every pot, do you suppose he meant a princely fowl like the capon? Possibly, but back in the late sixteenth century, simple barnyard scratchers were probably far more savorous than modern chickens. Certainly the commercially raised ones today are too flavorless for simple roasting, scarcely fit for the table of king or commoner. Roasted properly, capons seem to have a bit more flavor, with hints of the old barnyard variety—although perhaps it is just the extra care given to the preparation. At any rate, they make a fine main course and provide a worthy showcase for a good wine.

With capon, you may happily serve either white or red wine. Like turkey, it will accommodate both. The same goes for veal. In either case, if the preference is for white, the best choice is a medium-bodied Chardonnay like Saint-Véran, Rully or Montagny. With veal in cream sauce or chicken *vallée d'Auge* (cream sauce laced with calvados), a somewhat oakier Chardonnay would be better, a Meursault, for instance. With veal *piccata* and its altogether different flavor emphasis, however, a Sauvignon Blanc would be more complementary to the lemony accent in the veal, either one from California or one of the Loire Valley whites like Sancerre or Pouilly-Fumé. I often prefer a smooth red wine with veal *piccata*, perhaps an Italian Carmignano or Gattinara.

Stuffed breast of veal can handle a balanced red, as can the capon. I recommend a light Bordeaux, or at least a mature one that is smooth and round, without tannin. A well-balanced California Cabernet would also be a fine choice, although, again, not one that is too assertive, too full-bodied, or too tannic—Beaulieu Vineyard's Rutherford Cabernet, for instance. Consider also a Pinot Noir. Try one that emphasizes the variety's charming fruit, such as those of

Saintsbury or Acacia. Other possibilities: McDowell Valley Vineyards Syrah, Crozes-Hermitage (red), Morgon, Mercurey, Rioja, and Gattinara.

Spring's Ritual Feasts

Easter morning was almost as exciting as Christmas morning to me when I was growing up. I took great delight in looking for hidden eggs and was somewhat disappointed if they proved too easy to find. My sister, Beverly, and I spent the whole day hiding and rehiding eggs until the shells were so cracked we finally *had* to peel and eat them.

Easter was also memorable for the wonderful smell of homemade rolls wafting up from the kitchen below as I woke up. On special occasions throughout the year, my grandmother rose before dawn to begin making the mouth-melting pockets of buttery goodness that the whole family adored. Baked ham was the traditional Easter dinner at my house. Diamond-scored and studded with cloves, it went into the oven by 10:00 A.M. to roast slowly while we went off to church. The service was always longer than usual, as growling stomachs told us long before we sneaked a look at the time.

The prolonged exchange of greetings after church was really our small-town version of the Easter parade, a chance to see and be seen in new spring frocks and bonnets. To Beverly and me, it seemed to go on forever as the grown-ups ogled and dawdled; finally, just as we began to feel faint with hunger, it was home to the Easter table, adorned with the regal ham and its savory companions. There were times as little girls when my sister and I had to be coaxed to eat, but not on this gustatory occasion. We set to boldly, demolishing sizable helpings of cheese grits soufflé, my mother's special green bean casserole, the piquant relishes and condiments that invariably accent the Southern table, and, of course, my grandmother's wondrous rolls.

Wine was not served at our family table. Bourbon was the southern drink, but it was fresh-brewed iced tea at table. Consquently, it was not until I left home and came to live in New York that I experimented with different wines, trying to find one that would go well with ham. My husband, Bill, was from the South and also loved ham, so we had it fairly often in those early days of my limited kitchen capability. We tried several reds, whites, and rosés, mostly dry ones because we were sure, or so we had read, that only dry wines went with food. For me, however, the astringency of the red wines and acidity of whites like Graves, Sancerre, and Muscadet did not match up well with the salty savor of the ham. They left a bitter or metallic taste.

It was not until some years later that I discovered the wine that to my taste goes best with ham, the fruity, off-dry Blanc de Noirs made in California. The slight sweetness of most Pinot Noir Blanc, Cabernet Blanc, and white Zinfandel sets up the flavor of the ham instead of detracting from it. I also quite like a sparkling rosé with ham, something like Schramsberg Cuvée de Pinot Noir or Iron Horse Brut Rosé.

These wines also work quite well with other pork dishes, particularly those that include fruit, such as roast pork stuffed with prunes. An exception, perhaps, is roast suckling pig. You can, of course, serve the Blanc de Noirs with it, but I would prefer a sharp fruity young red like Dolcetto d'Alba or Freisa, or a light Burgundy such as Santenay, Bourgogne Rouge, or Côtes de Beaune-Villages.

What follow are menu ideas for spring entertaining.

KOSHER WINES

For centuries, the traditional Passover wine was a sweet, heavy red Malaga, or in this country one of the cream concords from Manischewitz and other producers of kosher wines. Many people still like to have a traditional sweet red on the Seder table for the ritual toasts, but also wish to serve drier, lighter wines that go better with food during the rest of the meal. Recognizing the growing interest in Jewish traditions, importers have expanded the availability of kosher wines to include dry, well-made table wines that complement the main Seder dish of chicken or beef brisket and suit the taste of more sophisticated wine drinkers.

Kosher wines are made basically the same way as nonkosher wines, although strict rules of hygiene are monitored more closely in the handling of the grapes and the wine. Most importantly, a rabbi must oversee every step of the wine-making process for a wine to be certified kosher.

Some of the most attractive kosher wines come from relatively new wineries in Israel, such as those of Yarden and Gamla. In the early eighties, they revolutionized the entire category of kosher wines, producing crisp, stylish Sauvignon Blanc and well-balanced Cabernet Sauvignon from vineyards in the Golan Heights.

Dozens of imported kosher wines are now available from almost every wine region in Europe. They include Bordeaux, Chianti, whites from the Loire Valley and Alsace, Côtes-du-Rhône, Beaujolais, Burgundy, Champagne, Asti *spumante*, and numerous others.

In California, Hagafen Cellars produces kosher Chardonnay, Cabernet Sauvignon, Riesling, and Pinot Noir Blanc. Hagafen wines (Hagafen means "the vine" in Hebrew) have been served in the White House when visitors who observe the dietary laws of Kashruth dine there.

Two wineries in Sonoma, Gan Eden and Weinstock, also produce attractive versions of these varietals as well as Gamay Beaujolais and white Zinfandel.

SPRING MENUS

I. SPRING DINNER

Cheese Straws	**BOUVET BRUT**
Vichyssoise	
Sautéed Shad with Its Roe **Green Peas à la Française**	**SAINT-VÉRAN**
Strawberry Mousse	**SWEET VOUVRAY**

MENU NOTES: Following the sparkling wine aperitif no wine is really needed with vichyssoise. With shad alone, grilled or sautéed, I would choose Sancerre or Sauvignon Blanc. With the roe, however, which is subtle but rich, I would choose a medium-bodied white Burgundy like Saint-Véran, Aligoté, Rully, or Pouilly-Fuissé. Light red wines can also accompany shad with roe—a cru Beaujolais such as Brouilly or Regnié, or a chilled young Bourgueil from the Loire. The creaminess in the dessert mousse softens the acidity of the strawberries, which by themselves might prove too tart even for sweet Vouvray.

II. SPRING DINNER

Duck Liver Pâté	RHEINGAU RIESLING KABINETT
Roast Capon Tortellini Salsa Verde Arugula Salad	POMEROL
Cheese: *Chèvre* French Bread	LE CIGARE VOLANT
Fresh Fruit	

MENU NOTES: The richness balanced with acidity in a *Kabinett* Riesling makes an attractive counterpoint to pâté for the first course. Pomerol, softest of the major Bordeaux reds, is excellent with roast fowl. California Merlots such as Rutherford Hill, Stag's Leap, Clos du Val, or Benziger could serve as worthy alternatives. The *chèvre* (goat cheese) and crusty French bread should clear away the tartness of the salad and then prove a fine partner to Le Cigare Volant, Bonny Doon's berryish blend of syrah, grenache, and mourvèdre.

III. SPRING LUNCHEON

Prosciutto and Melon	BRUT SPUMANTE
Pasta Primavera	GAVI DI GAVI
Cheese: Gorgonzola Dolcelatte	FREISA OR DOLCETTO
Pear Sorbet	POIRE WILHELM

MENU NOTES: This simple but festive lunch could also be a weekend brunch or Sunday supper. Gavi is one of Italy's best dry whites; the fruity reds of the Piedmont, Freisa, and Dolcetto d'Alba go well with the creamiest of Italy's blue Gorgonzola, *dolcelatte*. Poire Wilhelm, optional of course, is an eau-de-vie made from pears and is lovely with many types of sorbets.

IV. EASTER DINNER

Herb-Stuffed Mushroom Caps	APERITIFS
Baked Ham with Chutney Asparagus with Lemon Butter Cheese Grits Soufflé	SCHRAMSBERG CUVÉE DE PINOT NOIR
Ambrosia and Sponge Cake	MALMSEY MADEIRA

MENU NOTES: Any of several aperitifs are appropriate here, but dry sherry or a fresh white wine like Vouvray or Alsace Gewürztraminer is recommended. If you prefer not to serve sparkling wine with the main course, try a white Zinfandel, Pinot Noir Blanc, or chilled Beaujolais. Malmsey is the sweetest of the Madeiras and goes especially well with a simple sponge or pound cake.

Figs in Prosciutto	SANCERRE ROSÉ
Cheeses: Saint-Nectaire,	
Mimolette, Torta con	
Basilico	
French Bread	

Chocolate Cookies	COFFEE AND TEA

MENU NOTES: For a simple afternoon gathering (a meeting or just a social event), this mini-repast makes an attractive but easily prepared array. For ease of handling, wrap the figs in slices of prosciutto and secure with a toothpick. The cheeses are a complementary contrast to one another. Saint-Nectaire is a mild, pale yellow semisoft cheese; Mimolette is bright orange, firmer in texture, and somewhat stronger in flavor; Torta con Basilico is a piquant soft cheese with alternating layers of Gorgonzola and Mascarpone flavored with basil. Other choices might include *chèvre* in olive oil and herbs, Gruyère, Bavarian blue, and Port Salut. If Sancerre Rosé is not available, choose a light red like Beaujolais-Villages (serve lightly chilled), Gamay Beaujolais, or a fruity red like Bandol or Zinfandel.

Other spring dishes	*Suggested wines*
Asparagus	Dry Riesling, Sylvaner, dry Chenin Blanc
Baked Ham	Rosé, Riesling *Kabinett* or *Spätlese*, Brut Rosé, blush wines, *vin gris*
Baked or Poached Salmon, Plain or With Mild Sauce:	Oregon Pinot Gris

with richer sauce:	Meursault, Chassagne-Montrachet, Chardonnay, such as Trefethen, Chateau Montelena, Ste. Michelle Cold Creek
Capon, Roast	Pinot Noir, Pomerol
Fish *Pâté,* or Terrine	Riesling *Kabinett Halbtrocken* or other dry Riesling
Lamb Stew with Vegetables	Lighter Cabernet, Pomerol or Saint-Emilion, Cahors, Rioja Riserva
Pasta Alfredo	Chardonnay, such as Jermann, San Michele, Ruffino, Tocai Friulano
Pasta Primavera	Gavi, Pinot Blanc, Trentino, Chardonnay, dry Riesling
Paté	Dry Vouvray, Chinon or Bourgeuil, Sancerre Rouge
Shad, Sautéed or Broiled With Roe	Sauvignon Blanc, Saint-Véran, Viognier, cru Beaujolais
Veal Piccata	Sauvignon Blanc, medium-body red such as Gattinara, Ghemme, or Merlot

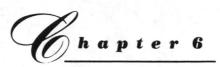

Chapter 6

SLAKING
SUMMER'S
THIRST

▼

*I hear the clink of bottles being carried to the well from
which they will be pulled up, cooled, for dinner to-night.
One of them, red-currant pink, will accompany the green
melon; the other, a sandgrown wine, amber-coloured and
over-generous, goes with the salad of tomatoes, pimentos
and onions soaked in oil, and with the ripe fruit.*

COLETTE, *La Naissance du Jour*

*S*ummer's easy days bring out the grill, the picnic hamper, the deck umbrella, the Mediterranean cottons that look so pretty on outdoor tables. . . . Vacation starts anew every Friday night as people head to the country, the beach, or simply out the back door to the patio. Of all the seasons, summer is more a state of mind than any other. Entertaining is more casual and informal this time of year—and quite probably more frequent, what with summer houses and weekend guests.

Summer wines are also more casual, and it is most useful to lay in a cache of bottles—three, six, or more cases, according to what you think you will need—to set up a summer cellar. Having wine at hand for the variety of impromptu occasions that present themselves is a practical convenience that is almost a necessity. The wines should, of course, be the sort that go with the foods of the season, which include light, often spicy, casual dishes such as salads, pâtés, quiche, barbecued meats, fresh fruits and vegetables, fish, shellfish and more fish, cold roast duck or chicken. Wines to go with such fare can be lighter and less complicated, too, although there should also be wines that can simply be sipped on their own. Briskly chilled whites and gently cooled reds are a boon to the palate on languid summer days.

The wines of summer linger in memory for me not because of their commanding character but for the sheer delight and refreshment they offer. After a day on the beach, I find nothing more welcoming than the gentle fizz of a wine spritzer or one of the cool, moss-tinted Rieslings from the Mosel. It is cooling just to look at them.

This season of light, refreshing drinks inspires one to get creative with cold foods. Picnics are no longer just sandwiches, cole slaw, potato chips, and cookies—unless it is just you and the kids. Today's picnic is a gastronomical affair as witnessed in New York at summer concerts in Central Park, at Tanglewood in Massachusetts, or the Hollywood Bowl in California. People get quite elaborate with their arrays of pâtés, caviar, pasta salads, smoked meats, laid out with colorful napery, wineglasses—even candelabra, for pete's sake.

Whether you choose to get that fancy or not, the picnic has been revised and revamped, in part due to travel abroad, where there is ample opportunity to take advantage of fabulous *charcuterie* in France, Italy, and Germany. In this country, wonderful prepared foods are available from the burgeoning number of specialty take-out shops. They can be a great substitute for dishes you haven't time to do yourself. I do recommend keeping the wines fairly simple for such alfresco dining, since there might well be several things to concentrate on aside from the music of Mozart or the glass in hand.

For a Fourth of July barbecue you might want to consider a wine punch like sangria if you are planning for a crowd. Cold punches are refreshing and infinitely stretchable or shrinkable depending upon the number coming. Champagne punch can add a festive note to summer gatherings, not to mention making it easier for people to get acquainted (and faster, too).

Stocking a Summer Wine Cellar

There are a number of different wines to consider stocking this time of year. They are not only marvelous to bring out after a steamy day at the beach, but perfect to take along as gifts to weekend hosts. The following list offers a more detailed consideration of wines to choose for a summer cellar. As a general rule, buy the youngest available vintage; most should be no older than a year or two. Store your wines in a cool place away from light.

MUSCADET

This crisp dry white from the western end of the Loire Valley is one we described in Chapter 5. Those who like shellfish will want to consider Muscadet as one of the lighter, less expensive wines to go with shrimp, clams, mussels, and other shellfish. It also makes a good aperitif wine.

RIESLING

Riesling, as consumers are beginning to discover, can be highly versatile with food. It is especially true of dry Rieslings from Alsace, the Pacific Northwest, New York, and *Halbtrocken* wines from Germany. And I have found it to be particularly accommodating to Oriental foods—Thai, Chinese, Vietnamese, Cambodian, Indian, and Indonesian (see Chapter 7). A four- or five-year-old Alsace Riesling, for example, can be one of the best all-around wines for fish, seafood, and chicken dishes, as well as certain vegetarian dishes (provided they are not too spicy hot, in which case beer or a mildly sweet blush wine would be better).

An off-dry or lightly sweet Riesling *(Kabinett, Spätlese Halbtrocken)* goes well with a surprising variety of foods as well. If there is any sort of light sweetness in the dish or its sauce, these wines will work better than the austerity of an Alsace Riesling. A dry or off-dry Riesling proves a good match for pastas with cream sauce, for instance. Crisp acidity balanced with a mere touch of sweetness cuts the richness of the sauce and blends well with the texture and creaminess.

Other matches for dry to off-dry Rieslings include numerous wursts, from hot dogs to the lordly *choucroute garnie a l'Alsacienne;* turkey; chicken breast, veal cutlet, rabbit in cream sauce; light fish such as trout, lemon or dover sole, flounder, sea bass (not, however, the stronger striped bass); quiche; leek and onion tart; smoked chicken or turkey salad; cheeses like Tilsit, double creams and creamy blues.

Sweet Rieslings labeled *Spätlese* or *Auslese* without the qualifying *Halbtrocken* are often very sweet yet balanced with the superb acidity that sets them apart from all but a few others. They are not merely sweeter, however, they have more character and complexity without sacrificing liveliness. The experience of a good *Spätlese*, which generally is lighter and somewhat less sweet than *Auslese*, is often like biting into fresh green apples, especially in wines from the Mosel.

On American Rieslings, the terms *White* or *Johannisberg* are used to denote the true German Riesling, to differentiate it from other varieties like Sylvaner, which are labeled Franken Riesling or Monterey Riesling. This to me is a lamentable practice that complicates the name unnecessarily. Riesling is Riesling; it is all other varieties that should be qualified. In this book, Riesling is the true German Riesling unless otherwise stated.

While California makes attractive Rieslings, particularly among the light, early-harvest versions that have a springlike freshness, it is elsewhere that American Riesling is beginning to shine. The cooler growing regions of the Northwest (Washington and Oregon), New York (the Finger Lakes), and west Texas now produce dry and off-dry Rieslings with scintillating fruit and acidity. A few examples: Hogue Schwartzmann Vineyard, Chateau Ste. Michelle, Hermann Wiemer, Dr. Konstantin Frank, Llano Estacado. From California some of the best include Joseph Phelps, Clos du Bois, Chateau St. Jean, Firestone, Fetzer, Mark West, Louis M. Martini, Jekel, Masson Vineyards, Smith-Madrone, and Trefethen.

California's late-harvest Rieslings, particularly those affected by the mold known as *Botrytis* (see Glossary), are widely regarded as among the best made anywhere. These sweet, golden wines, redolent of peaches or apricots coated with honey, are rich enough to serve as dessert in themselves, or perhaps accompanied only by ripe summer fruit. Leading producers of these wines are Joseph Phelps, Chateau Saint Jean, Freemark Abbey, Firestone, Navarro and Robert Mondavi.

GEWÜRTRAMINER

The first time I ever tasted Gewürztraminer I got quite a shock. The sweet spice aroma had led me to expect a sweet wine. What a surprise to find it breathlessly dry. The wine was from Alsace and, like Alsace Riesling, very dry indeed. Gewürztraminer is a wine that people either hate or grow to love. Given a chance, its compelling spicy perfume becomes very seductive, and if matched with the right food, the wine is superb. In Alsace, they drink Gewürztraminer, especially richer, late-harvest ones labeled *Vendange tardive,* with foie gras and other rich liver pâtés. This is a classy combination; the richness of goose (or duck) is beautifully offset by the spiciness and brisk acidity of the wine.

Gewürztraminer, especially the dry Alsace version, is difficult to match with other foods. It is invariably recommended with Oriental dishes, especially Chinese, and I did so myself in the earlier version of this book. I have rarely found Gewürztraminer to be as satisfying, however, as dry Riesling—except perhaps with deep-fried foods, like General Tso's Chicken, and dishes flavored with ginger or Szechuan heat. It quite overpowers subtler dishes.

California Gewurztraminers tend to be sweeter and less spicy than those of Alsace, but when balanced with good acidity they can be charming to sip on their own or serve as aperitifs. Louis M. Martini, however, makes a good dry Gewurztraminer, one that goes very well with food. Other Gewurztraminers to look for are included in the following list.

Recommended wines: Alsace: Leon Beyer, Dopff & Irion, Marcel Deiss, Hugel, Klug, Domaine Weinbach, Willm, Zind-Humbrecht; American: Chateau St. Jean, Clos du Bois, Columbia, DeLoach, Firestone, Fetzer, Grand Cru, Llano Estacado, Mark West, Louis M. Martini, Navarro, Palmer, St. Francis, Tewksbury, Tualatin.

SAUVIGNON BLANC

This is another excellent choice for fish and shellfish because of its somewhat citruslike or flinty character. The Sauvignon Blancs of the Loire Valley, Sancerre, and Pouilly-Fumé, as well as many California Fumé Blancs, have a sharp, distinctive aroma that is often described as "grassy." This is a descriptive term wine tasters use to convey the wine's assertive, herbaceous character, rather like the clean, fresh scent of new-mown grass or hay. A bit of it is very attractive, although some wines from France and California occasionally have it to excess.

The names Sauvignon Blanc and Fumé Blanc are interchangeable in California. Both are dry wines, though nowadays there is a trend to mild sweetness that I deplore. More often than not, those labeled Fumé Blanc are straight varietals with a pronounced grassy character. Many of those labeled Sauvignon Blanc have a somewhat fuller, rounder style produced from techniques like barrel fermentation or blending in Sémillon, which adds extra flavor dimension to Sauvignon Blanc and gives it the depth to age beyond a year or so. Several California wineries now blend nearly equal parts of these two varieties, such as Concannon Assemblage, Inglenook Gravion, Kendall-Jackson Chevrier Blanc, and Vichon Chevrignon.

Sauvignon Blancs, whether labeled as such or as Fumé Blanc or with a proprietary name, have greatly improved in recent years. The aggressively herbacious character is tamed with more attractive fruit and better balance. The wines wonderfully complement the slightly smoky flavor of grilled fish or shellfish. They are also excellent with the likes of soft-shell crab, broiled or sautéed, shad and its roe, swordfish, and shark marinated in a soy-lime sauce.

Though light reds are appropriate, and even preferable, with meaty fish like salmon, tuna, or bluefish, those who prefer a white wine will find Sauvignon Blanc the likeliest choice. Cold poached salmon is better served by a crisp Sauvignon, particularly with dill or hollandaise sauce, as are salmon steaks in a spicy marinade.

One caveat is boiled shrimp. This is perhaps a very personal preference, but I find Chardonnay—almost any style of Chardonnay, from Mâcon Blanc to Meursault to Grgich Hills or Fetzer Sundial—much more compatible with a mess of boiled shrimp than Sauvignon Blanc. I discovered this from Dallas wine consultant Rebecca Murphy, who gives a shrimp-and-Chardonnay party every spring. Becky prepares a bushel of steamed shrimp, plus gulf crab if it's available, grilled vegetables, and salad. The guests, wine buffs all, each bring a bottle of Chardonnay, with the wines running the gamut in appellation—Burgundy, Chablis, Australia, California, Texas. Oaked or unoaked, Chardonnay fruit brings out the best in simple boiled shrimp. The faint sweetness and succulence of the meat needs the rounder, fuller fruit of Chardonnay. Most

Sauvignon Blanc is too acidic and one-dimensional (though it works better with the smoky accent of grilled shrimp).

Sauvignon Blanc's versatility extends to a wide variety of other foods, however, most notably those with a Mediterranean flavor. With their base of olive oil, garlic, and tomatoes, and the strong accent of herbs like thyme, rosemary, savory, and tarragon, Mediterranean dishes are well matched with the minerally character of Sancerre, the citrusy flavor of Fumé Blanc. For similar reasons, wines made from Sauvignon can handle other strongly flavored foods, such as those of the southwest with their tangy salsas and barbecue sauce, Greek and Middle Eastern foods, as well as a variety of Indian curries.

One other food should be mentioned: goat cheese. Goat cheese is a classic match with Sancerre, the two just by themselves, and maybe a warm, crisp baguette. When goat cheese is an important component of salads, pastas, or other dishes, other Sauvignons or Fumés—or Sancerre—will often be the only wines that taste right.

Wines to consider: Sancerre; Pouilly-Fumé; Menetou de Salon; Sauvignon de Touraine; Fumé Blanc: Chateau Saint Jean, Dry Creek, Ferrari-Carano, Glen Ellen, Iron Horse, Robert Mondavi, McDowell, Preston Cuvée de Fumé; Sauvignon Blanc: Adler Fels, Alderbrook, Brander, Concannon, Kenwood, Robert Pepi, Preston, Silverado, Stag's Leap Wine Cellars, Sterling, St. Clement, Simi. Blends: Carmenet, Concannon, de Lorimier, Flora Springs, Inglenook, Merryvale, Vichon.

CHARDONNAY

The intense, distinctive fruit of chardonnay produces some of the biggest, most full-bodied, and powerful of dry white wines. They go beautifully with many types of food but best suit fish and shellfish. The lighter ones from southern Burgundy around Mâcon are agreeable with practically anything that is not overly pungent or spicy, and refreshing just by themselves as aperitifs. A great favorite among Burgundy lovers is Saint-Véran, which is fuller and somewhat richer than simple Mâcon, yet only a few dollars more in price. Some Pouilly-Fuissé has also dropped in price to a level much more in line with its quality.

Along the Côte d'Or, as the best vineyard area in Burgundy is known, white Burgundies are bigger, richer wines. There is the brilliant, steely elegance of Corton-Charlemagne, the softer, more supple Meursault, and the intriguing complexity of the Montrachets. These wines, with their largesse of fruit and generous proportions, can be supreme with fish, chicken or veal in *beurre blanc*. To the north in Chablis, Chardonnay becomes dry as flint, with a bracing acidity that makes it the perfect complement to platters of our ocean-fresh cherrystone or littleneck clams.

Chardonnay is California's best white, a wine of opulent fruit and heady fragrance. Styles of Chardonnay have taken new directions in recent years, away from ponderous alcohols—although many of them are still big, powerful wines—and overzealous use of oak for aging. The best wines of recent vintages show more balance and finesse, but still possess that great burst of fruit that makes them irresistible.

California winemakers continue to try different ways of handling Chardonnay. This is all to the good, but it can be trying for the wine lover. As winemakers have sought a better balance of ripe fruit and acidity and exercised a more restrained use of oak barrels for aging—surely a laudable course—many of the wines unfortunately exhibit a boring sameness and lack of the individuality one looks for in wines that aim for greatness. Let us hope this is only a temporary sacrifice toward new achievement.

There are, nonetheless, a number of Chardonnays that have established a track record for excellence. Consistently good California ones are by Trefethen, Freemark Abbey, Robert Mondavi, Chalone, Acacia, Chateau Montelena, Mayacamas, Grgich Hills, Chateau Saint Jean, Burgess, Kistler, Morgan, Au Bon Climat, Chappellet, William Hill, Saintsbury Reserve, Sanford, Sonoma-Cutrer, Sterling, Iron Horse, and Simi. These wines and the whites of Burgundy are superb choices for such summer fish specialties as whole poached cold salmon, lobster, filets of bass, swordfish, pompano, or red snapper.

Other white wines to consider stocking for summer are light California wines like Pinot Blanc and dry Chenin Blanc, and some of the most appealing Italian whites from the country's northeastern regions. Pinot Grigio, for example, is bracingly dry and crisp and goes well with shellfish. Light and fragrant Chardonnays and Pinot Biancos are some of the best bargains around; most of them can be found for under $10 a bottle.

Rosés

These unsung wines have become such clichés that they are now a woefully neglected segment of wine production. I like a good dry rosé in summer or anytime, but they are hard to come by. Certain French rosés are quite pleasant, particularly drier ones like Tavel and the brisk rosés from Provence that are more frequently available now.

For a time in California, there was a rush to make rosés out of surplus red grapes—cabernet sauvignon, pinot noir, zinfandel, and petite sirah. These varietal rosés are still made, but by fewer wineries and have mostly given way to blush wines and, happily, the dry *vin gris*.

Vin Gris

Blanc de Noirs have given rise to another style that is increasingly seen from California, *vin gris*. This term originated in France for pale-colored dry wines made from red grapes. In California, too, it stands for pink wines that are quite dry, to distinguish them from other blush wines that are lightly sweet or off-dry. They are simply delightful, although not widely available as yet. I hope this category will grow. Alas, however, it is one of those names that sounds sophisticated and high-falutin' and thus is liable to be snatched up and used for any sort of pale wine, dry or not. I hope this does not happen; in the meantime, look for such good ones as Chalone, Saintsbury, Sanford, Bonny Doon, Joseph Phelps, and McDowell.

Light Reds

Several red wines are worth considering to go with summer's grilled meats and barbecue. Beaujolais is a natural for summer. The lighter ones, like simple Beaujolais or Beaujolais-Villages, take very well to light chilling and are, in fact, much fresher and livelier when chilled. They should not be as cold as white wine; about thirty minutes in the refrigerator or fifteen minutes in an ice bucket will do it.

The bigger Beaujolais are those with village names: Brouilly, Chiroubles, Regnié, Côte de Brouilly, Saint-Amour, Fleurie, Juliénas, Chénas, Morgon, and Moulin-à-Vent, listed more or less in ascending order of richness and body. Brouilly is the lightest and can be gently cooled, but the others may be served as any other red table wine, at 65 or 70 degrees. The bigger ones, like Morgon and Moulin-à-Vent, are excellent with almost any sort of food from barbecued hamburgers to grilled steak or lamb.

Americans who feel a surge of patriotism on the Fourth of July may well want to go American in choosing wine for Independence Day cookouts and picnics. The ideal choice for such an occasion is one of California's berry-ripe Zinfandels, intensely fruity wines that can handle hearty barbecued meats. Zinfandel used to come in so many different styles that one never knew what to expect until the cork was pulled. Some were light and fruity like Beaujolais, others were dense and tannic and overpoweringly alcoholic. Zinfandels still run a gamut of styles, as discussed earlier in Chapter 3. Sturdy, chewy ones continue to be popular, but the best Zinfandels are more balanced and stylish. Their abundance of ripe fruit flavors—often reminiscent of raspberries or blackberries—makes them a delicious quaff. Names to seek out: Ridge, Preston, Burgess, Clos du Val, Storybook Mountain, DeLoach, Kendall-Jackson, Kenwood, Quivira, Ravenswood, Shenandoah, Dry Creek and Sutter Home.

Other light reds to consider for summer include Gamay Beaujolais, Freisa, and Dolcetto d'Alba, richly fruity reds from the Piedmont region of Italy, the Valtellina reds such as Grumello and Inferno, Spanish Riojas, Gamay Beaujolais from California, Côtes du Rhône, Cahors, as well as the lighter, moderate-priced Bordeaux and California Cabernets, which tend to be lighter in style.

SPARKLING WINES

My refrigerator is never without a bottle of bubbly in summer, any of several inexpensive ones like Domaine Chandon or Lembey Brut, but a champagne as well. I need little urging to unleash the effervescence, and I find it is particularly handy to have it chilled and ready for any eventuality, like suddenly discovering it is someone's birthday or anniversary. Sparkling wine is also my most frequent choice as an aperitif.

SERIOUS REDS

Connoisseurs do not necessarily set aside great reds just because the weather is warm. Air-conditioning maintains an atmosphere in which such wines can be enjoyed even in the warm months. Still, if the weather outside is steamy, as it is likely to be anywhere from New York to Houston, it does not feel good to consume heavy reds and then step out into boiler-room temperatures. California's coastal regions, by contrast, drop considerably in temperature at night. It can be 80 degrees or higher at noon and 60 degrees by nightfall, comfortable enough to enjoy fine Cabernets and Zinfandels or Bordeaux that might be better with a good cheese than with a heavy meat dish. Such a dinner might well feature fish as the main course, accompanied by Chardonnay or white Burgundy.

The menus for summer that follow are mostly informal, like the season itself.

SUMMER MENUS

I. FOURTH OF JULY BARBECUE

Miniature Grilled Sausages	SANGRIA
Charcoal-Broiled Steaks	ZINFANDEL
Grilled Red Peppers and	
** Zucchini**	
Warm Potato Salad	
** Vinaigrette**	
Corn on the Cob	
Peach Cobbler with Hard	ICED COFFEE
** Sauce**	

MENU NOTES: Some people might want to drink sangria throughout this mini-fiesta, so be sure to have enough ingredients to expand the mixture if need be (see page 168 for the recipe). If you prefer something drier, this is a perfect opportunity for a *Vin Gris* such as Sanford, or a dry rosé like Sancerre or Marsannay. Zinfandel is the quintessential American red, but other good choices would be Beaujolais, Gamay, Cabernet Sauvignon, or Merlot.

II. SUMMER DINNER

Deviled Crab Canapés	**KIR ROYAL**
Filets of Striped Bass with Tarragon Butter **Steamed New Potatoes** **Green Beans with Mushrooms**	**CORTON-CHARLEMAGNE**
Compote of Summer Berries	**MOSCATO**
Shortbread Cookies	**ESPRESSO**

MENU NOTES: Kir Royal is the traditional kir made with Champagne (see page 160 for the recipe) and an elegant prelude to dinner. The cold soup needs no wine and serves as a transition to the main course and its wine. Corton-Charlemagne is one of the grander white Burgundies; other choices would include *premier cru* Puligny-Montrachet or a rich California Chardonnay such as Robert Mondavi Reserve, Au Bon Climat, Chalone, Freemark Abbey, or Morgan. Sweet Moscatos such as Louis M. Martini Moscato Amabile, Mondavi Moscato d'Oro, Fetzer Muscat Canelli, and Bonny Doon Vin de Glacière Muscat are delectable with fresh blueberries, strawberries, or raspberries.

III. CONCERT-UNDER-THE-STARS PICNIC

Carpaccio Cylinders **Deviled Eggs** **Rigatoni Salad Provençale** **Eggplant Caviar** **Chicken Salad with Coriander and Pine Nuts** **Plum Tart**	**VIN GRIS OR DRY ROSÉ SUCH AS DOMAINE TEMPIER**

MENU NOTES: This portable feast is not unlike some of the tony repasts unveiled at summer concerts in Central Park's Sheep Meadow, but it can travel anywhere. Carpaccio is thinly sliced, very rare roast beef, here rolled in convenient cylinders; add a horseradish–sour cream dressing for a bit more zest, if you like. A blush wine such as white Zinfandel can substitue for drier pinks if you prefer something sweet.

IV. LUNCHEON ON THE TERRACE

Spicy Tomato Aspic	**BLOODY MARYS**
Sliced Duck Breast Salad with Green Beans and Zucchini **Corn Fritters***	**BEAUJOLAIS-VILLAGES**
Homemade Blackberry Ice Cream with Blackberry Liqueur	**COFFEE**

MENU NOTES: This is the only recipe that recommends a nonwine drink, simply because almost any wine would fight with the piquant flavors of tomato aspic, a beautiful and cool summer dish. The Beaujolais is best lightly chilled. The best blackberry liqueur is the German Echte Kroatzebeere, made with wild blackberries from the Black Forest.

Other Summer Dishes	*Suggested Wines*
Bouillabaisse	Tavel, Provençal Rosé; Marsanne

*See Ann Clark's *Fabulous Fish*.

Barbecued Chicken	Côtes-du-Rhône, Syrah, Beaujolais-Villages
Cold Poached Salmon	Dry Riesling, French Chablis, Pinot Gris
Grilled Salmon	Pinot Noir, Red Burgundy
Fried Calamari	Pinot Grigio, Gavi, Soave
Chicken Vindaloo	Dolcetto d'Alba (lightly chilled), Grignolino Rosé
Goat Cheese Marinated in Olive Oil and Herbs	Sancerre
Grilled Sardines	Chateau Simone Palette Rosé; Sanford Vin Gris
Grilled Polenta with Fontina	Orvieto
with Goat Cheese	Fumé Blanc
with Gorgonzola	Dolcetto, Lambrusco, light Zinfandel
Grilled Vegetables with Aioli	Dry Rosé, such as Domaine Tempier
Ham, Baked or Smoked	*Vin Gris*, blush or *rosé*
Pasta with Shellfish	Gavi, Vernaccia, Pinot Grigio, Fiano di Avellino
Prosciutto di Parma	Galestro, Monte Vertine Bianco, Sablet Blanc
Salade Nicoise	Tavel, Provençal Rosé
Shish Kabab	Merlot, Zinfandel, Gigondas, Cabernet
Smoked Duck with Green Lentil Sald	Sancerre, rouge or rosé
Steamed Mussels with Shallots and White Wine	Muscadet Sèvre et Maine
Stuffed Grape Leaves and Tabouli Salad	Roditys, Boutari Retsina
Watercress, Leek, and Potato Soup (hot or cold)	Entre-Deux-Mers

*C*hapter 7

A
WORLD OF
CUISINES

▾

In my experience it is the countryman who is the real
gourmet and for good reason; it is he who has cultivated,
raised, hunted or fished the raw materials and has made
the wine himself.

PENELOPE GRAY, *Honey from a Weed*

$\mathcal{O}$ne of the most dramatic developments during the eighties was the explosion of interest in ethnic cuisines. I use the term "ethnic" guardedly because it is somewhat demeaning, apt only in that it immediately connotes a realm of food from certain regions of the world—the Orient, the Mediterranean, the Middle East. Ethnic indeed, in our eyes only! These cuisines are all much older than our own, and in some instances more keenly refined.

The world of cuisine is growing smaller—or larger, depending upon how you look at it. More communication among chefs of different nationalities makes it seem smaller in one sense, but the fabric as a whole is growing larger, with all the additions and adaptations that are taking place almost worldwide today. There are tremendous cross-cultural influences—the French-Vietnamese exchange, for example; Japan's innovative ways with western foods; Latin America's mingle of European and indigenous native ingredients; Germany's new continental (and largely French) accents. In America, true to our melting-pot heritage, we have adopted them all. They have become integrated with our own traditions and regional specialties, part of the patchwork quilt of American cuisine that is still evolving. It is an exciting time to be eating and cooking . . . and drinking wine.

A decade ago, wine recommendations for various world cuisines were so general as to be quite useless. Imagine making the blanket recommendation of Gewürztraminer for Oriental food; it *does* work

141

for certain dishes, as noted later, but we have come much farther in our appreciation of the subtlety and variations in Far Eastern cuisines since the first edition of this book. In this chapter we briefly explore some of the cuisines and culinary influences that are most popular in this country and discuss the considerable variety of wines that can accompany them.

There seem to be two schools of thought regarding wines with Asian foods. Some people prefer strongly flavored wines that can "stand up" to the assertive flavors of Asian dishes, which is why Gewürztraminer often gets a blanket recommendation. Others, however, prefer wines that are subtle and support a dish rather than contrast with it. As in all matters of taste, both approaches are perfectly valid, even at the same table.

I love Oriental foods of all types—Chinese, Thai, Vietnamese, Indonesian, Indian, Japanese—with their multitude of intriguing flavors that are by turns savory, sweet, spicy, tangy, fruity, sour, mildly hot to blistering. To allow interplay with the complex flavors found in so many Asian dishes, I generally choose wines that are restrained in flavor but still have character.

If I had to choose a single wine to serve with a variety of Chinese dishes, for example, it would be three- to five-year-old Alsace Riesling. On many occasions I have been thoroughly delighted with how these crisp, firmly balanced wines perform. There is a good reason for choosing a Riesling with a little age on it. In younger Rieslings, the acidity can be too aggressive for the food (though one likes that with rich, deep-fried foods). In older Riesling, the acidity melds into the wine, making it smooth and round rather than angular. German *Kabinett* Rieslings of this age also work well with many Oriental dishes, as do dry Rieslings from the Pacific Northwest. Dry Italian white wines—Gavi, Soave Classico, Vernaccia, Orvieto, Pinot Grigio—also go surprisingly well. Crisp, simple, and fruity, they can be very agreeable, if unremarkable.

It is a mistake, of course, to force a single type of wine to "go with everything." Asian dishes, with their broad range of flavors and accents, deserve much more consideration. For example, Vietnamese specialties made with the pungent *nuoc mam* (or *cham*) sauce, the salty baste made with fermented anchovies, call for something assertive, like Alsace Gewürztraminer, Sauvignon Blanc, even Champagne. When Champagne shipper Veuve Clicquot teamed up with Nicole Routhier, author of *The Foods of Vietnam*, Clicquot nonvintage Brut was a great hit with the spicy spring and shrimp rolls, Goi Cuon, and Cha Gio Tom. Later in the meal the pungent beef stew, Thit Bo Kho, proved a splendid match with Clicquot's Brut Rosé.

Nor should one forsake reds with Oriental foods. Red wines best suit Peking duck and other duck dishes, as well as hearty meat dishes. Often, however, Asian meat dishes de-emphasize their "meatiness" when ground, shredded, and combined with vegetables. These dishes go perfectly well with mild-flavored dry whites.

The suggestions below are, admittedly, fairly general in most instances, but useful as a starting point for what can become an intriguing game of matchup.

Chinese dishes, for instance, are big on ginger, Hoisin, chili pepper, nuts, and mushroom. A few examples are these:

Steamed Fish (Sea bass, sea trout, snapper)	Dry Riesling, Pinot Blanc, Chardonnay (lightly oaked or unoaked), Gavi
Moo Shu Pork	Off-dry Riesling, blush wines, Soave, dry rosé such as Taurasi Irpinia
Peking Duck	Full-bodied Pinot Noir; Zinfandel
General Tso's Chicken (deep-fried)	Alsace Gewürztraminer, sparkling wine; Crémant d'Alsace
Beef with Vegetables	Light fruity red, or sturdier Côtes-du-Rhône, depending on richness of sauce; dry white (Pinot Blanc) or dry rosé

Lemon Chicken	Citrusy Sauvignon Blanc, such as Ferrari-Carano, Matanzas Creek, Simi
Chicken or Shrimp with Almonds or Cashews	Dry Riesling, Pinot Blanc, Gavi, light Chardonnays
Szechuan, Hunan (hot and spicy)	Blush wines, off-dry Riesling or Chenin Blanc
Prawns, Lobster	Chardonnay
with chilis:	Sauvignon Blanc
deep-fried:	Sauvignon Blanc, Gavi
Sweet and Sour	Difficult, but melony Sauvignon such as Silverado can handle; try Spanish sparkling *cavas*
Vegetarian (vegetables, bean curd)	mild and fruity white such as Trebbiano, Soave, Gamay (chilled), or blush

Thai

Thai cuisine has a reputation for being intense, and it can be. But it is also somewhat simpler than Chinese food, more cleanly defined, at any rate. In many Thai dishes one or two accents predominate—fresh coriander, for instance, coconut milk, or peanut sauce—though some can be pungent with chili. I find white wines that are dry but fairly mild in flavor to be best suited to most Thai dishes, even those incorporating beef, which loses some of its red meat character to coconut or peanut sauces. Pinot Grigio can work quite nicely here. With shrimp or chicken accented with fresh coriander (cilantro, Chinese parsley), try Sancerre. For spicy hot dishes, an off-dry blush or rosé can be soothing as well as complementary, as can chillable reds. If chilis are not present (or not overpowering) in red meat dishes, real reds are in order—a good Beaune or Washington Merlot with Thai duck, for instance, a full-bodied Rhône with beef or pork in a savory sauce.

WINES: Pinot Blanc, Orvieto, Soave Classico, white Zinfandel,

Sancerre; Gamay Beaujolais (chilled); red Burgundy, Merlot, Saint-Joseph, or Châteauneuf-du-Pape.

Vietnamese

Vietnam has been called a culinary crossroads, with over a thousand years of influence from other cultures—China, India, France. The food of Vietnam today is Oriental with a French flair, and it is the French influence that makes it so compatible with wine, more so, perhaps, than any other cuisine of the Orient. Here is a cuisine where intense, assertive wines like spicy Alsace Gewürztraminer and Sauvignon Blanc are needed to handle, for instance, the pungent savor of *nuoc mam* (or *cham*) sauce.

Subtler Vietnamese dishes, or those only mildly laced with the fish sauce, shine with dry Riesling, again the firm, crisp Alsace version being my first pick. Alsace Gewürztraminer, on the other hand, is better with spare ribs marinated in *nuoc mam*, stuffed crab, or a tangy shrimp/chicken/beef fondue. And, of course, there is always Champagne—Brut or Blanc de Blancs with spicy *nuoc mam* specialties, Brut Rosé with savory duck and beef dishes.

Milder meat dishes are perfectly appropriate with medium-bodied red wines like Pomerol, Saint-Emilion, Cahors, or California Cabernet or Merlot—not mightily tannic ones, however; smooth and fruity with moderately firm structure works best.

WINES: Alsace Riesling or Gewürztraminer, German Riesling *Kabinett*, Sauvignon Blanc, Champagne; Pomerol, Saint-Emilion, Cahors, less-than-intense Cabernet or Merlot.

Indian/Afghani

These cuisines—flavored with cumin, curry, saffron, chilis, clove, ginger, and other spices—are not as difficult for wine as one might think. The most versatile wines with Indian food are firm, dry rosés, such as those from the Rhône and Provence, or full-bodied *vin gris* from California. But one can get much more specific. Sauvignon Blanc works superbly with shrimp or chicken curry, tandoori chicken, or Afghan Aushak. Try a *cru* Beaujolais like Morgon with lamb biryani, and with fiery chicken vindaloo, the fruitiness of a young, lightly chilled Dolcetto d'Alba. Understated whites like Pinot Blanc, Pinot Gris, or Gavi can support a variety of chicken, pork, fish, and herby rice pilaf.

Lamb dishes range from the rather simple but savory *roghan josh* (Pinot Noir, Merlot) to hearty roast or grilled meats with richer sauces that call for bigger reds like Barbaresco, Rioja Riserva, or Gigondas. Other suggestions include:

Pakoras, Samosas	Sparkling wine, Brut or Brut Rosé
Biryani Shahjahani (saffron rice with lamb)	Merlot, Saint-Emilion, dry rosé from Tavel or Provence
Dhansak (lamb with curried vegetables)	Beaujolais (chilled) or Dolcetto
Grilled Lamb Kabobs	Châteauneuf-du-Pape, Zinfandel, Merlot
Jhinga Kari (shrimp curry)	Sauvignon Blanc
Kheema Biryani (Ground lamb with pilaf)	Rioja Riserva
Pakta Machli (Baked fish with coriander sauce)	Riesling *Kabinett*, Italian Chardonnay
Murg Tikka (ground chicken curry)	Sancerre, Pinot Blanc
Leg of Lamb Mughlai	Saint-Emilion, Barbaresco
Tandoori Chicken	Saint-Véran, Sauvignon Blanc, Greco di Tufo
Vindaloo	Crisp blush wine such as white Zinfandel, or *vin gris*

Japanese

Japanese food is generally milder than other Oriental cuisines, except for sushi and sashimi, which are spiced with the fabulously tangy green horseradish known as *wasabi*. Despite the piquant horseradish, sushi is faintly sweet and is well served by off-dry

Riesling, light crisp whites like Galestro or Gavi, or fruity sparkling wines from Spain, the Loire Valley, or California.

Complex, assertive wines are difficult with many Japanese foods, especially those that include dipping sauces, usually a combination of tamari (soy sauce), lemon or lime and miso (fermented bean curd), vinegar, and pickle. These piquant accents for relatively bland foods call for crisp wines high in acidity but somewhat neutral in flavor—one reason beer is a popular accompaniment for many foods. Sake is more interesting to sip as an aperitif than with most foods. Wines like dry Riesling, Pinot Gris (or Grigio), Baden Weiss-burgunder, Sylvaner, and Pinot Blanc, however, can be useful with mild dishes; Sauvignon Blanc if the flavor accent is citrus, lightly sweet Riesling or chillable red if tamari is dominant.

Mediterranean

Mediterranean food includes the cooking of Provence and other parts of southern France, Spanish Catalan, and coastal Italy. The dishes of this region are high in tomatoes, garlic, olive oil, aioli, black olives, and herbs such as rosemary, basil, oregano, fennel, and thyme. It includes grilled or roasted meats and vegetables, ragouts, stews, tagines, cassoulet, bouillabaisse, bourride—dishes with strong, often earthy, flavors.

The wines that go best with these are frequently those that have evolved in the region—the reds and dry rosés of the Rhône, Provence, and the Midi, and the Penedés in Spain (but also Rioja). We can also look to Italian reds like Barbera, Chianti, even Montepulciano d'Abruzzo (despite its Aegean locale).

The most versatile white with such foods, however, seems not to be local wines but Sauvignon Blanc. Its grassy, herby, citrusy flavors and high acidity stand up well to the olive oil that is the base of most Mediterranean cooking. Crisp, minerally Rhône whites also work, but my quarrel with these wines is that they are inconsistent, often oversulphured and with a baked taste that is not pleasant. The Rhône's best simple whites come from Lirac, Sablet, and Rasteau. The region's top whites—Condrieu, Beaucastel's Chateauneuf-du-Pape Blanc—are expensive but can be superb with Provençal-style fish or chicken dishes.

Californians experimenting with Rhône varietals (syrah, mourvèdre, grenache, cinsaut for reds, roussanne, viognier and marsanne for whites) include Bonny Doon, Calera, Cline, Edmunds St. John, McDowell, Joseph Phelps, Preston, Qupé, Ritchie Creek, and William Wheeler.

RED WINES: Provence (Bandol, Cassis, Côtes de Provence), Rhône (especially Cotes-du-Rhône, Côtes-du-Rhône-Villages, Vacqueyras, Lirac, Rasteau, Sablet, Cairanne, Gigondas, Saint-Joseph and Châteauneuf-du-Pape), Midi (Corbières, Côtes du Roussillon, Fitou, Minervois, Madiran), Cahors; Spanish reds from Rioja, Penedés, Navarra; Barbera d'Alba, Chianti, Montepulciano d'Abruzzo; California Syrah, Mourvèdre, or Rhône varietal blends like Côtes Sauvage, Oakley Cuvée, Clos de Gilroy, or Le Cigare Volant.

ROSÉ WINES: *Vin Gris*, dry rosés from Provence or the Rhône, Italy, Rioja.

WHITE WINES: Sablet Blanc, Lirac Blanc, Châteauneuf-du-Pape Blanc, Cassis, Bellet; Condrieu; Gavi, Galestro; Rueda; Qupé Marsanne, Bonny Doon Le Sophiste, California Viognier.

Middle East

With its flavorings of cumin, cinnamon, oregano, clove, and black pepper, Middle Eastern foods are best served by fruity dry rosés and by light chillable reds such as Gamay Beaujolais. Greece is now producing some excellent dry whites and fruity red wines under the Boutari label that go admirably with many of these foods. Sauvignon Blanc can handle most dishes that include or are accompanied by feta cheese, as well as lemony stuffed grape leaves, hummus, and baba ghannouj.

Provençal rosé works superbly with couscous, vegetable or chicken, even lamb or beef, though light red wines like Côtes-du-

Rhône, Rioja, Fitou, or Côtes du Roussillon may better suit the meat. Savory stewed lamb in its numerous variations needs a red with hearty fruit but not overly tannic, like the Greek Naoussa or a Portuguese red from the Alentejo, or a Spanish red like Gran Sangre de Toro or Toro Colegiata. Shish kebab and roast kid call for a sturdier red from the Rhône or Provence, Australian Shiraz, or California Mourvèdre.

Mexico and the Southwest

These foods have become favorites throughout the United States. There are distinctions to be made among these foods as far as wine is concerned, more so all the time, in fact, since creative chefs are constantly inventing or adapting imaginative variations on the basics: Tex-Mex, grilled meats and vegetables, salsas, herbs like cilantro and basil.

With Mexican food, especially Tex-Mex, Corona beer may still be *numero uno*, but there is a good reason why sangria, an iced wine drink, evolved locally: It's a mouth-soothing antidote to the fire of chilis. It remains an excellent choice, refreshing and cooling, especially if it is on the drier side (see recipe on page 168). Blush wines, well-chilled, serve the same purpose.

Accents of the Southwest—cilantro, lemon and lime, barbecue sauce (sweet or fiery), tomatoes, chilis, green and red peppers— flavor all sorts of foods, from fish to chicken to beef and pork or lamb. Unless chilis force a choice of blush wine or beer, the guidelines for wine are similar to what they are for these foods in more familiar contexts: sturdy reds for beef, lamb, or game; Sauvignon Blanc for spicy fish; oaky Chardonnays for shellfish; light, fruity reds for pork and some chicken and for meaty fish like tuna.

Chapter 8

GATHERINGS LARGE AND SMALL

▼

Fill the goblet again! for I never before

Felt the glow which now gladdens my heart to its core;

Let us drink!—who would not?—since, through life's varied round,

In the goblet alone no deception is found.

LORD BYRON

*H*olidays are always occasions for gatherings, be they large or small, and wine, nowadays, is a major part of them. Increasingly so, according to some wine merchants, whose regular customers sometimes arrange to return unused bottles after a large party. "Most of the time," one retailer told me, "the unopened bottles of liquor come back, but the wine never does."

Wine considerations are quite different for the large party. Take the open house, for instance. The hosts may want to have a full bar if the crowd is large and varied, but there are sure to be numerous requests for wine, both red and white. This is the perfect time to call on the metric magnums (1.5 liters). The best value and most convenient size for home use, in my view, is the metric magnum. Larger sizes are awkward to manage—try pouring from a giant three- or four-liter bottle. You will find that what you have saved in cost is lost in spillage as you try to wield the clumsy things.

Better-quality wines also come in magnums. We are lucky today that a global wine glut has loosed a flood of better-than-average wine onto the bulk market, much of which is used to spruce up simple *vin de table,* putting it several cuts above the mediocre plonk of yesteryear. While there is still plenty of that available, pass it up and try the better ones. Some of them, surprisingly, cost little more than the cheap ones.

Many of the moderate-priced imports come in magnums. Are you tired of the ubiquitous Soave? I am, I admit, but I am pleased to be able to turn to such agreeable Italian white wines as Pinot Grigio, Chardonnay, and Pinot Bianco, which are now bottled in magnums. Many of the premium wineries of California produce not only generic blends of interesting flavor but also with varietal wines. By definition, varietal wines must contain at least 75 percent of the grape variety named on the label. Among the better ones are Robert Mondavi, Fetzer, Woodbridge, Round Hill, Domaine St. George, M. G. Vallejo, J. Moreau, Los Vascos, and Glen Ellen Proprietor's Reserve, made mostly of Cabernet Sauvignon. Good generics are also made by Raymond Pedroncelli, Prosper Maufoux, and Georges Duboeuf. Each of these producers also makes generic wines, which, incidentally, are those blended from several grapes rather than a single dominant one.

Zip Code Wines

I have found considerable variation in quality among some of the imported wines available in magnums, particularly the French brands. These generic blends fall under the government designation *vin de table* but are often referred to as "zip code" wines. This is because they have no specific appellation of origin, only a zip code of the shipper's headquarters. Even the name of the town is not permitted (such as Beaune or Mâcon) so that consumers will not mistakenly infer that the wine comes from there. While it may have, the producer is permitted to use grapes (or wine) from anywhere in France. To some extent, this accounts for the inconsistency from bottle to bottle that some wines exhibit.

These wines go by such proprietary names as Boucheron, Partager, Rene Junot, Sommelière, and many others. The wines are not vintage-dated, so one has no idea if the bottle purchased today is the same batch of wine that was in a previous bottle. The blends change depending on the grapes available, and that is why Boucheron Blanc de Blancs, for example, tastes fresh and agreeable sometimes and old, flat, or somewhat oxidized at others. Fortunately, intense competition within the import market has forced the French to become more conscientious about the quality of these wines, but it is still a good idea to try a bottle before you stock up for a party.

The following is a list of quality jugs to consider when you must buy in quantity. The extra character in these wines perks up mixed drinks based on wine like spritzers; in punches, however, it will simply be lost so you may use something cheaper. Incidentally, very light reds like Valpolicella, Bardolino, and others taste insipid at room temperature. Unfortunately, they are usually served this way at restaurants. Chilling these wines makes them a bit snappier.

Red

Boucheron Cuvée Rouge
Casal Thaulero Red
Domaine St. George
Fetzer Premium Red
Georges Duboeuf
Jaboulet La Table du Roy
La Vieille Ferme Rouge
Maître d'Estournel Bordeaux
  Rouge
Meribeau Rouge
Michel Lynch Rouge
Robert Mondavi Vintage Red
The Monterey Uyd Classic
  Red
Moreau Rouge
Parducci Vintage Red
Prosper Maufoux Cuvée Rouge
Riverside Farm Zinfandel
Round Hill House Cabernet
Sebastiani Country Cabernet
  Sauvignon

White and Rosé

Aliança Rosé
Casal Thaulero Trebbiano
Cavit Pinot Grigio
Chevalier de Védrines
Georges Duboeuf Chardonnay
La Vieille Ferme Blanc
Robert Mondavi-Woodbridge
  Sauvignon Blanc,
  Chardonnay, White
  Zinfandel
Moreau Blanc
M.G. Vallejo Chardonnay
Parducci Vintage White
Rene Junot Blanc
Round Hill House
  Chardonnay, Fumé Blanc
Wente Bros. Grey Riesling

STOCKING THE HOLIDAY BARS

Impromptu gatherings during the holidays make a well-stocked bar a must. For planned occasions, figure on the basis of how many drinks each bottle serves. If you have invited twenty people for cocktails, for example, you will need at least four bottles of liquor and half a case of wine. An intimate dinner for six will call for a similar amount of wine but the mix will be different: a bottle or two of sparkling wine for aperitifs, three bottles for the meal itself, and a dessert wine or vintage port after. If possible, estimate your holiday needs in advance and buy all at once. Prices are usually lower by the case, and in many areas the store will deliver, saving you the hassle of running out at a hectic time.

The average mixed drink contains one and a half ounces of liquor (a jigger) and about four ounces of mixer. Calculate at a rate of one and a half drinks per person per hour for cocktail parties.

	Servings per Bottle
COCKTAILS, MIXED DRINKS *(1.5 ounces liquor)*	
750 milliliters (25.4 ounces)	16
1 liter (33.8 ounces)	22
1.75 liters (59.2 ounces)	39
TABLE AND SPARKLING WINES *(4 ounces)*	
750 milliliters (25.4 ounces)	6
1 liter (33.8 ounces)	8
3 liters (101 ounces)	25
4 liters (135 ounces)	32 to 33

Scotch, bourbon, and gin are the basics for any bar, but today the popular spirits are vodka, rum, and tequila, especially among the younger set. You should know your friends' preferences best; and they may run to Canadian, rye, or Irish whiskey. Larger sizes are the most economical, but the liter and 1.75-liter sizes are easiest to handle and will probably account for less spillage.

Be sure to have enough wine on hand, both red and white; check the list of recommended jug wines on page 155.

MIXERS Figure on about four ounces of mixer with the average cocktail or mixed drink, a bit more for highballs. Quart and liter sizes are the easiest to handle and store.

Basics:	club soda
	tonic water
	ginger ale
	cola
Fruit Juices:	orange
	pineapple
	tomato
	other (apricot, mango, cranberry)
Specialty Items:	Angostura bitters
	Rose's Lime Juice
	Triple Sec
	pearl onions
	olives
	sugar
	egg whites
	fresh lemons and limes
	grenadine
	crème de cassis
	dry and sweet vermouth
For After Dinner:	cognac
	armagnac
	calvados
	eaux-de-vie (poire, framboise, kirsch, mirabelle)
	liqueurs

Bar Tools:	cocktail shaker
	jiggers
	ice bucket
	bar spoons
	swizzle sticks
	strainer
	assorted glasses and stemware
	zester
	corkscrew
	bottle opener
	cocktail napkins

Wine Cocktails

For parties or as aperitifs before a meal, you can break the monotony of the simple glass of white or red wine with a wine cocktail. Wine mixes easily with soda, fruit juices, fortified wines like vermouth, and various brandies. Probably the best-known wine cocktail is the spritzer, which is nothing more than a few ounces of wine, topped with club soda and a bit of lime or lemon.

Widely popular before meals is the kir—a drop or two of crème de cassis (black currant liqueur) with chilled dry white wine. The kir originated in Burgundy, where this libation was long known as *vin blanc cassis*. It was the favorite drink of Canon Félix Kir, beloved mayor of Dijon, revered for his resistance work during World War II. After his death, the drink was rechristened as his namesake. Aligoté, the lesser dry white wine of the region, was the wine used to make it; white Burgundy was considered too sacrosanct to adulterate. Today, any sort of dry white wine can be used, but the best choices are fuller-bodied whites like Aligoté (now much higher in quality as well as more stylish), Mâcon Blanc, or Pinot Blanc.

There are numerous variations on the kir. The Kir Royal substitutes sparkling wine or Champagne for the white wine. In place of the cassis, some people like to use other liqueurs, such as framboise or blackberry, or framboise eau-de-vie. What follow are a few wine-based mixed drinks to stimulate your taste buds—and your imagination. Perhaps they will inspire creations of your own.

Note: All bottles are the regular 750-milliliter size unless otherwise noted.

▽

SPRITZER

Makes 1

2 to 4 ounces red or white wine
2 ounces sparkling water or club soda
Wedge of lime or lemon

Pour wine over ice cubes in a balloon-shaped wineglass; fill with Perrier, Pellegrino, or other sparkling water. Garnish with a wedge of lime or lemon.

▽

WINE COOLER

Makes 1

4 ounces dry red or white wine
2 ounces pineapple juice, chilled
1 teaspoon lemon juice
Sparkling water (optional)
Wedge of lime

Combine first three ingredients over ice in a wine goblet. Fill with sparkling water, if desired, and garnish with lime wedge.

▽

KIR (VIN BLANC CASSIS)

Makes 1

½ teaspoon (less or more to taste) crème de cassis
4 to 6 ounces Aligoté, Mâcon Blanc, or Pinot Blanc

Pour the cassis into a 10-ounce wineglass; add thoroughly chilled white wine. Do not stir. In classic form, the kir is neither served over ice nor garnished with lemon zest. As the drink is consumed it gets sweeter toward the end, where the cassis is concentrated, and more white wine may be added, if desired.

▽

KIR ROYAL

Makes 1

½ teaspoon (less or more to taste) crème de cassis
4 ounces sparkling wine or Champagne

Pour the cassis into a tall flute or tulip-shaped glass and add chilled sparkling wine or Champagne.

Note: Substitute framboise liqueur or eau-de-vie or blackberry liqueur for the cassis as a variation of this drink.

▽

CARDINAL

Makes 1

This is a kir made with red wine. Originally it was called the *communard* around Lyon, but it was renamed for euphemistic reasons to free it of political associations. It is a delightful change of pace from the white wine kir.

½ teaspoon crème de cassis
4 ounces Beaujolais-Villages, chilled

Pour cassis into a 10-ounce wine goblet and add the Beaujolais. A couple of ice cubes will keep the drink fresh and sprightly.

▽

CHAMPAGNE COCKTAIL

Makes 1

1 lump sugar
Angostura bitters
Champagne
Lemon peel

Place sugar lump in the bottom of a Champagne glass; dribble Angostura on top of it and add chilled Champagne. Do not stir. Garnish with the slice of citrus.

▽

MIMOSA

Makes 1

2 ounces orange juice
2 ounces Champagne or other sparkling wine, chilled
Fresh mint leaves (optional)

Mix the orange juice and Champagne in tall flute or tulip-shaped glass. In the South, mimosas are often garnished with fresh mint leaves in summer.

▽

CARIBBEAN SUNSET

Makes 1

1 teaspoon Cointreau
Dash of orange bitters
3 ounces red wine
Club soda
Lemon or orange peel

Pour the Cointreau and bitters over ice in a large wineglass; add the wine and fill with club soda. Stir and garnish with lemon or orange peel.

▽

SEABREEZE

Makes 1

1 teaspoon Poire Wilhelm
4 ounces sparkling wine

Pour Poire Wilhelm into a tall flute or tulip-shaped wineglass, and fill with chilled sparkling wine. Do not stir or the bubbles will dissipate.

▽

VALENTINE

Makes 1

3 ounces Beaujolais
1 teaspoon Boggs Cranberry Liqueur
Cranberry juice cocktail

Combine ingredients with ice in a cocktail shaker and stir or shake until well chilled. Strain into wine goblets.

▽

AMERICANO

Makes 1

1½ ounces Campari
2 ounces sweet vermouth
4 ounces club soda
Orange peel

Combine the Campari and sweet vermouth over ice in an 8-ounce wine goblet; add the club soda and garnish with orange peel.

▽

CINZANO

Makes 1

3 ounces Cinzano or other dry vermouth
¼ teaspoon Angostura bitters
¼ teaspoon orange bitters
Orange peel

Combine the Cinzano and bitters with ice in a cocktail pitcher and stir until thoroughly mixed and chilled; then strain into a 4-ounce wineglass or cocktail glass. Garnish with orange peel.

Punches

One way to stretch wines for large gatherings of twenty or so is to serve punches. There are several good ones based on wine, ranging from simple sangria to classics like Fish House or Bishop's Punch. The United States has a long tradition of punches, going back to colonial days. Early cookbooks contain recipes for many types of punches, creamy syllabubs (white wine, sherry, and cream) and specialties like the New Orleans *coup de milieu* (frozen champagne and fruit punch) served during Mardi Gras. Punches are easy on the host because they are simple to make, and easy on the guests because they can serve themselves. Many punches can be made a day ahead and chilled overnight, then poured over a block of ice in the punch bowl at party time. This is not possible with Champagne punches, however, since they would lose their sparkle in the process. Champagne or carbonated beverages must be added only at the last moment, otherwise the bubbles will disappear.

Most punches are cold, which makes them particularly refreshing in warm weather. By all means, consider punch for summer holiday outings. Punches made with still wine are even portable for picnics.

(You could take along the Champagne, pop the cork when everything is set up, and add it to the fruits and juices in the thermos or cooler.) At indoor parties, the punch bowl is always a center of activity, and therefore a good icebreaker and a place where strangers can get acquainted easily.

Cold punches were popular in the South where I grew up. Now that I live where the frigid winds of winter are in full force by December, I often enjoy hot drinks. One of my favorites is *glögg,* which I first had at the home of a Swedish friend one Christmas Eve. Each year, Ingrid would invite a small group of friends to a Christmas supper of traditional Scandinavian dishes—*lutfisk* (dried codfish with cream sauce and nutmeg), caramelized potatoes, Swedish meatballs, and limpa, the marvelous sweet dark Swedish rye bread, spread with Swedish butter. We drank our Christmas toasts with Ingrid's special version of *julglögg,* a spicy mulled wine that I have made many times since (see page 169 for the recipe).

That was my first Christmas Eve in New York and it had a magic all its own. Outside, great wet flakes of snow floated down and covered the city in white. It was a stunning sight for me. New York is never prettier than in the first moments of snowfall, when a damp mist halos every streetlamp and cafés glimmer with a warmth more inviting than usual. When we left at midnight it was still snowing, but we scarcely felt the cold. We walked all the way home, some forty blocks, bathed in the glow of snow crystals and radiant city lights. Of course, we were somewhat aglow ourselves, warmed from toes to fingertips with *glögg.*

Here are some of my favorite punches:

▽

THE WASSAIL BOWL

Makes 10 to 12 4-ounce servings

The original old Saxon Wassail was usually made with ale, although sherry, known in Merrie Olde England as Sack, was also used. Many versions exist. This one is pieced together from several old recipes with deliciously satisfying results.

1/4 teaspoon freshly grated nutmeg
2 to 3 cloves
2 sticks cinnamon
1/4 teaspoon ground cardamom
1/4 teaspoon powdered ginger
1 cup water
2 bottles medium-dry sherry
1/3 cup brandy
1 cup sugar
3 egg yolks
6 egg whites
6 medium-sized baked apples

In a large saucepan, simmer the spices gently in the cup of water for 10 minutes. Add sherry, brandy, and sugar; heat, but do not boil. Mix the egg yolks with 1 cup of the warmed sherry mixture and pour into a punch bowl. Gradually add the remaining hot sherry. Immediately beat in the egg whites with a whisk until the mixture is frothy. Garnish with the baked apples, which will float on the surface. Serve while still warm.

▽

CHRISTMAS PUNCH

Makes 20 4-ounce servings

1½ cups extrafine sugar
1½ cups water
6 strips lemon peel
10 to 12 cloves
2 sticks cinnamon
5 medium-sized pears, diced
2 cups orange juice
1/2 cup lemon juice
2 bottles medium-light red wine
1/2 cup brandy (optional)

1 lemon, sliced
1 orange, sliced

Combine the sugar, water, lemon peel, spices, and pears in a large saucepan and bring to a boil; simmer for 5 minutes or until the liquid is a light syrup. Cool and put through a strainer. Then add orange juice, lemon juice, wine, and brandy. Mix well and pour over a block of ice in a large punch bowl. Garnish with slices of lemon and orange.

▽

CHAMPAGNE PUNCH

Makes 30 4-ounce servings

2 bottles dry white wine
1 quart grapefruit juice
1 fresh pineapple, diced and crushed in blender
2 bottles Champagne or sparkling wine

Combine the white wine, grapefruit juice, and crushed pineapple. Pour the mixture over a block of ice in a large punch bowl. Add Champagne just before serving.

▽

SOUTHERN REB PUNCH

Makes 30 4-ounce servings

1 pint brandy
1 pint bourbon
1 quart club soda
12-ounce can pineapple juice concentrate
½ cup freshly squeezed lemon juice
2 ounces grenadine
2 bottles sparkling rosé

Combine all the ingredients except the sparkling wine and mix well. Chill and pour over a block of ice in a large punch bowl. Add the rosé just before serving.

▽

FISH HOUSE PUNCH

Makes 25 4-ounce servings

Fish House Punch originated at a men's club in Philadelphia in the mid-eighteenth century. The original recipe was a heady potion that contained no wine, but countless modifications of the recipe exist today. This one substitutes wine for some of the hard liquor, but it is still a potent brew.

> *½ cup extrafine sugar*
> *2 cups lemon juice*
> *1 bottle peach brandy*
> *1 bottle golden rum*
> *2 bottles dry white wine*
> *1 quart club soda*

Dissolve the sugar in the lemon juice and brandy; then add the rum and white wine. You may refrigerate the mixture a day ahead at this point, if desired. Pour over a large block of ice in a punch bowl; add club soda just before serving.

▽

CLARET CUP

Makes 25 4-ounce servings

This venerable red-wine punch dates at least to the seventeenth century in England and was a popular libation in colonial days as well as throughout the old South. Claret is the English term for red Bordeaux, but any dry red wine may be used.

> *2 bottles dry red wine*
> *½ cup blackberry brandy*

> 2 tablespoons grenadine
> ½ cup Cointreau (or Triple Sec)
> 1 quart club soda
> Juice of 3 lemons and 3 oranges
> 1 pineapple, crushed in blender
> Slices of fresh fruit (oranges, peaches, strawberries,
>   papaya)

Combine liquid ingredients and pour the mixture over a block of ice in a large punch bowl. Garnish with the sliced fresh fruit.

▽

SANGRIA

Makes about 1 quart

This drink, which originated in Spain, is very popular during warm weather, especially with spicy foods like Mexican. As is the case with most punches, the ingredients are variable and optional. This recipe calls for red wine, but white wine or rosé may also be used. For brunches or luncheons, you may want a lighter beverage, so omit the brandy.

> 1 bottle Rioja red wine
> 1 ounce brandy or vodka (or to taste)
> Juice of ½ lemon
> Juice of ½ orange
> ¼ cup extrafine sugar
> 8 to 10 ounces Perrier or club soda
> Lemon and orange slices

Combine first six ingredients with ice cubes in a large pitcher; stir thoroughly. Garnish with lemon and orange slices. For sweeter sangria, increase the amount of sugar.

▽

SWEDISH GLÖGG

Makes about 8 6-ounce servings

With a nod of thanks to Ingrid Svensson, who gave me my first (and best) *glögg*.

> **2 bottles dry red wine**
> **½ cup extrafine sugar**
> **6 to 10 cloves**
> **2 sticks cinnamon**
> **2 tablespoons cognac (or to taste)**
> **Raisins**
> **Slivered almonds**
> **Additional sticks cinnamon, for garnish**

Combine the red wine, sugar, cloves, 2 cinnamon sticks, and cognac in a heavy saucepan or stockpot. Warm over medium heat to just below boiling, but do *not* boil. In punch cups or coffee mugs, place a few raisins and slivered almonds, and pour in the piping hot liquid. As an extra touch, add a cinnamon stick, which can be used for stirring, to each mug.

▽

MULLED WINE

Makes 4 6-ounce servings

This warming drink is known by various names, *gluhwein* or *vin chaud; glögg* is a somewhat more elaborate version of it.

> **1 bottle red wine**
> **¼ cup extrafine sugar**
> **Juice of 1 lemon**
> **4 or 5 cloves**
> **2 sticks cinnamon (or ¼ teaspoon ground cinnamon)**
> **Dash of brandy**

Combine ingredients in a heavy saucepan and heat gently until the mixture just starts to simmer. Remove from heat and serve in mugs.

▽

BISHOP'S PUNCH

Makes 12 4-ounce servings

4 oranges stuck with cloves
2 bottles sweet red port
½ cup cognac
¼ teaspoon each ground cinnamon, nutmeg, and
  mace

Bake the clove-studded oranges on a cookie sheet in a 350-degree oven until soft and just oozing juice. Remove them from the oven and set aside. Heat the port, cognac, and spices in a large saucepan until steam vapor rises from it, but do not boil. Place the oranges in a large ceramic bowl and add the heated wine. Serve in punch cups or mugs.

▽

BOSCOBEL MULLED CIDER

Makes about 20 6-ounce servings

Christmas celebrations often include whole families, so it is nice to have a festive drink for the youngsters in the crowd. Boscobel, a nineteenth-century mansion built near the Hudson River at Garrison, New York, offers candlelight tours for the public at Christmastime, ending with cookies and mulled cider in the mansion's open-hearth kitchen.

2 gallons fresh apple cider
2 whole lemons, sliced
2 whole oranges, sliced
8–10 cinnamon sticks

1 tablespoon ground cinnamon
1 tablespoon ground nutmeg
10 cloves

Combine all the ingredients in a large pot, heat just to boiling, and serve. For adult gatherings, use a cider wine such as Purpom and add 1 cup light rum or apple brandy such as calvados.

Chapter 9

FLOURISHING
FINISHES

▼

*For Port, red Port, is incomparable when good. It is not a
wine-of-all-work like Sherry. . . . It has not the almost
feminine grace of Claret; the transcendental qualities of
Burgundy and Madeira; the immediate inspiration of
Champagne. But it strengthens while it gladdens as no
other wine can do.*

GEORGE SAINTSBURY

*T*he serving of after-dinner drinks adds the final touch to a special dinner. These may include fortified wines such as port, Madeira, or sweet sherry; brandies such as cognac, armagnac, or calvados; or any of the white brandies known as eaux-de-vie, such as framboise, kirsch, mirabelle, or poire. Snifters of old rum, single-malt Scotch, or any number of liqueurs such as Grand Marnier, Chartreuse, or Benedictine may also be offered. After a succession of several wines, however, it is probably not a good idea to serve grain liquor. As mentioned earlier in Chapter 2, the mix of grape and grain is not the most felicitous combination, as your head may rudely announce to you (and not in a whisper!) the next morning.

Postprandial drinks have a special role at late-evening gatherings. I once held a "Come By After" party, inviting people to drop by after theater, after dinner, or after a concert, whatever their evening activity happened to be. I had a selection of ports, Stilton cheese and fresh fruit, a wheel of dry Monterey Jack, oloroso sherry for the holiday fruitcake, as well as single-cask cognac, armagnac, and single-malt Scotch. Since it was the week before Christmas, I had also chilled several bottles of Champagne. Those who had not had dinner started with that, accompanied by walnut pâté and crudités, and then went on to port or brandy. It was something different for a change and people seemed to have a lot of fun focusing on drinks that sometimes get overlooked when the party starts earlier in the evening. A few people even seemed to make some new discoveries.

Fortified Wines

Fortified wines are those that have been "fortified" with brandy, usually to a potency of 16 to 20 percent alcohol. Of the fortified wines, port is closest to the wine lover's heart. Many a wine dinner is structured with the express design of leading up to a carefully decanted vintage port as the stellar wine of the evening. Port is an excellent way to end the meal. Its sweet, potent strength goes superbly with a rich cheese like Stilton or aged farm Cheddar. It is frequently served just by itself, accompanied by nothing more than a dry biscuit, perhaps a bit of green apple or dried fruit, and walnuts. What you serve it with depends largely on the type of port—ruby, tawny, or vintage.

Port has been the Englishman's wine since the eighteenth century, when the English were forced to forgo claret and Burgundy because of import duties imposed on French products. Looking elsewhere for a satisfactory substitute, they found it in a red wine from the Douro region of northern Portugal, transported by riverboat to Oporto, the city at the mouth of the Douro River. Fortified with brandy to stabilize it for the voyage to England, it was eventually found to be more palatable if the brandy was added while the wine still had residual sweetness. The various styles of port, or *oporto*, as the Portuguese government would prefer us to call it, were developed to please the English palate, and, indeed, it is a wine admirably suited for the English climate and the chilly rooms of English manor houses.

Until recently, little attention was paid to port in this country, except by a few knowledgeable collectors. In the minds of many Americans it was known only as the cheap stuff guzzled on skid row. This so-called port was, however, made by California bulk-wine producers, with no claim to distinction whatever. In the past few years, port from Portugal has begun to enjoy a much wider audience as Americans have become familiar with the real thing. Prices for good port, especially vintage port, have risen with the increasing demand.

Wood Port

Wood port, mainly ruby and tawny, is aged in wood cask and ready to drink when bottled. It is less august than vintage port and less expensive, except perhaps for very fine old tawny ports that have aged in wood for many years. Ruby port is young and vibrant. It is required by law to age only three years before bottling, although some exceptional ones may be aged five or six, sometimes longer. They have some of the character of a vintage port, but not the depth or complexity. Some of the best are Fonseca Bin 27, Sandeman Founder's Reserve, and Cockburn's Reserve.

Tawny port traditionally spent much longer in wood—seven, ten, even fifteen years or more, its color gradually fading to a golden tawny; hence its name. Today, unfortunately, too many ports labeled tawny are young rubies with their color lightened by the addition of white port. Naturally, they do not possess the subtle complexity of genuine wood-aged tawny ports, which are more difficult to come by these days. For that reason, I often serve a good ruby such as those just mentioned. They make an excellent accompaniment to Stilton or other full-flavored cheese. Genuine tawny is delicious by itself; briefly chilled, it makes a wonderful aperitif or late-afternoon quaff. After dinner, tawny is fine with light cake or a sweet biscuit and dried fruit and nuts.

Vintage Port

More tradition and ritual surround the serving and drinking of vintage port than any other wine. To put it another way, more fuss is made over it. It is not a wine to pull out at a moment's whim. For one thing, it must always be decanted, unless it is very young, in which case it should only be opened for tasting purposes. It will offer no pleasure for drinking, certainly, until its aggressive, harsh alcohol and tannins have softened and mellowed. It takes at least twenty years for a good vintage port to reach maturity, sometimes much longer for the biggest vintages.

Most port, over 90 percent of it, is a blend of vintages that are aged in wood casks. Vintage port, however, is aged in bottle. When the grapes of a particular harvest are especially ripe and flavorful, the port shippers "declare" a vintage. The wines are kept separate and bottled within two to two and a half years, with the vintage date appearing on the bottle. Vintage port has enormous concentration, intensity, and depth. At first, it is dark, pitch black in some cases, because of the quantity of tannin. As the wine matures, the color lightens gradually and the tannins are thrown off in deposit. It is the heavy sediment in vintage port that necessitates decanting. Sometimes the cork is so encrusted with mold and accumulated sediment that the wine must be decanted through a cloth filter, such as muslin or double-layered cheesecloth. In very old ports, the cork may crumble as it is removed and bits of it may even get into the wine. Depending on its age and vigor, port needs considerable breathing time, usually a minimum of three hours for a twenty-year-old vintage port, but sometimes longer.

Vintage port is usually served after the meal at wine dinners. The dishes and glasses are cleared and the decanter of port brought out. It has been traditional, particularly among the English, to adjourn to another room entirely for serving port so that any lingering food smells from dinner do not interfere with its pristine enjoyment. This and a number of other rituals associated with the serving of port evolved in Oporto, Portugal, at The Factory House, an exclusive club for members of the British port trade. In *Wines and Spirits*, author Alec Waugh describes lunch at The Factory House, to which he had been invited as an honored guest:

> Forty of us sat down to an admirable, straightforward dinner. As an aperitif we had a dry white port; with our fish we had a white Graves; then a Pontet-Canet 1929. Cheese straws cleaned the palate for a tawny port. According to the menu we were then to weigh the respective merits of two vintage ports, a 1917 and a 1927. The names of the shippers were not given; it might have led to invidious comparisons. The chairman rose to his feet. We could not, he told us, appreciate the bouquet of vintage port in an atmosphere tainted with the fumes of food. We were invited to move into an adjoining room, taking our napkins with us. In that room, a second table awaited us, again set with 40 places.
>
> It was a lovely sight: a gleaming stretch of mahogany, a cluster of chandeliers, high piles of fruit, bowls of red roses,

cut-glass decanters. There was a Doulton dessert service, and a cherry-colored carpet to match. It was a delight to the eye, but that pleasure was slight in comparison with the enchanting assault upon one's nostrils of a cool, fresh room, scented with fruit and flowers. It was one of the most acute physical sensations of my life, but I am not sure that the port tasted any better.

The Factory House is also responsible for the custom of passing the port decanter to the left, clockwise. The origin of this practice is somewhat obscure, although many conjectures have been put forth. At any rate, it is considered a grave breach of etiquette not "to follow the sun" in passing the port. The host begins by serving the guest to his right, then himself, then he passes the decanter to his left. Each guest must keep the decanter moving, always to the left, until it is back in front of the host, who may then start it around again. Once everyone is served, the host raises his glass in a toast and then the guests sip at leisure.

In years that are almost but not quite good enough to be declared vintages, producers may offer what is known as late-bottled vintage, or LBV. It is made from the grapes of a single year, but it is bottled after four of five years rather than two, as is vintage port. LBV can be very enjoyable, and while it does not have the force and character of true vintage port, it is usually very good value.

Port lovers can become exceedingly involved in the intricate differences in ports of different vintages from the various shippers. There are light vintages that mature sooner, such as 1975, or big, heavy ones such as 1955 or 1963 (the latter is just beginning to show some of its wonders). Then there are the various "house styles." Taylor, for example, is known for wines of great depth and dense color, Warre for its distinctive bouquet, Croft for its fruit and body, Graham for its finesse, Quinta do Noval for its accessible fruit. One of the reasons for the increasing interest in vintage port is that it is such a safe and good value. By its very nature, vintage port is a superior wine, simply because it is only made in superior vintages. As long as it is properly stored, it is guaranteed to give pleasure as well as increase in value. If you compare current prices for the 1963s, for example, against those for the latest declared vintage, you will see why it can be a wise investment.

SHERRY AND MADEIRA

Both of these wines are greatly underrated today. The modern trend with sherry seems to be to serve it on the rocks or use it for cooking, either of which seems a waste of its unique character and the time and effort the Spanish take in putting it there. The popularity of certain medium-sweet sherries like Dry Sack, Dry Fly, and Croft's Original Pale Cream indicates a trend away from the heavily sweet cream sherries, but I would hate to see them pass away altogether. The rich luxuriance of wines such as Sandeman's Armada Cream, Emilio Lustau Rare Cream, Gonzalez Byass Nectar Cream, or even the well-known Harvey's Bristol Cream makes them lovely for sipping by themselves, or as an accompaniment to ice cream or dried fruits.

The drier sherries, fino and manzanilla, make fine aperitifs or afternoon wines. They are lighter in body than the other styles of sherry and taste best when chilled. They go superbly with salty or oily hors d'oeuvres such as olives, salted nuts, and smoked fish. I also like amontillado sherry, which is slightly less dry than fino or manzanilla, what we would call off-dry. Somewhat weightier is dry oloroso sherry. All cream sherries are olorosos to begin with, darker, fuller in body, and quite dry. They are sweetened to varying degrees with the addition of concentrated sweet wines made from very ripe grapes. Dry olorosos are very popular in Spain, both before dinner and sometimes after, but they have not been available here until recently. A few—such as Sandeman Royal Corregidor, Domecq, and Emilio Lustau—can now be found in the United States.

Madeira's problem is that it is even less well known than sherry, despite the fact that Madeira was one of the most popular drinks among the early American colonists, particularly those who settled in Maryland, Virginia, the Carolinas, and Georgia. "I drank Madeira at a great rate," wrote John Adams, and he was not alone among our early presidents to have done so.

The wine comes from the island of Madeira, off the coast of Portugal, and it is noted for its exceptional staying power. There are Madeiras dating back to the eighteenth century that are reputedly still in good condition. Today it is possible to buy Madeiras made from blends, or *soleras,* that were started in the late 1800s (we were served the Solera 1880 with the soup at the Bienstock dinner; see page 34), and these wines can be exceptional.

While Madeira and sherry are often mentioned in the same breath, as if they were interchangeable, they are nothing alike. If you do not care for sherry, do not assume that you will not warm to Madeira—or the other way around. Madeira has unusual acidity for a sweet wine; this gives it a refinement of structure around which the sweetness drapes itself with remarkable grace and subtlety. The sweetest Madeiras are as luxuriant as the sweetest sherries, but that edge of acidity gives them a more buoyant finish than sweet sherry, or even vintage port. That thrilling balance of sweetness and acidity is what captures the Madeira fancier, who can get quite rhapsodic about it. "I know no wine of its class that can beat Madeira when at its best," wrote the Englishman George Saintsbury. "The very finest Sherries of the luscious kind—even 'Bristol Milk' and 'Bristol Cream' themselves—cannot touch it."

There are several styles of Madeira. Sercial is the driest, excellent as an aperitif or by the occasional solitary glass. Verdelho, richer and off-dry—that is, with a touch of sweetness that is really more rich than sweet—serves a similar purpose. Rainwater is the name given to paler, drier verdelho, although it too may have an extra touch of sweetness but makes a very refined aperitif. Bual (sometimes called boal) is sweet and darker, more of an after-dinner wine. It is not, however, as sweet and concentrated as Malmsey. Malmsey is often recommended with cake, but the distinctive character of its sweetness—exceedingly rich but not in the least cloying—is something that I really like simply on its own. I do, however, think it absolutely stunning with plain, un-iced angel food cake.

Brandy

Brandy might be said to be the apotheosis of wine, the juice of the grape carried to its ultimate expression, its essence distilled.

It comes out of the still in pristine form as colorless eau-de-vie—water of life—a fiery liquid that must be tamed and tempered in oak to give it character and distinction. Strictly speaking, brandy is distilled from wine, which distinguishes it from grain-based liquors of similar strength. Calvados, however, is distilled from apples; white brandies, or eaux-de-vie like framboise and kirsch, are distilled from raspberries and cherries or other fruits. They are distinguished from fruit cordials such as blackberry or strawberry by the fact that they are colorless and breathlessly dry rather than sweet, as all cordials are.

Cognac is the most famous of all the brandies. It is made in the west of France around the town of Cognac, for which it is named. Most other wine regions, in Spain, Greece, and many other places, produce brandies distilled from wine. Practically any country that makes wine distills some of it into brandy.

COGNAC

There are many interesting cognacs available now, many of them from small individual shippers. The largest cognac shippers—Hennessy, Martell, Remy Martin, and Courvoisier are the best known—produce several levels of cognac. Age is the principal determinant of price and quality in cognac. The age of a brandy refers to the amount of time spent in wood cask, since once the spirit is bottled it does not change further. Cognac is aged in Limousin oak puncheons that give the brandy much of its distinctiveness. It is illegal to use dates or specific ages for cognac because precise figures would be difficult to substantiate. Approximate age is indicated by symbols or special words.

The youngest cognac is three-star, aged about three years. It is intended more for mixing than for anything else, to be used in cocktails or long drinks such as brandy and soda. VS (which stands for very superior) is another designation for three-star.

The next level, VSOP (very superior old pale), is used to signify cognacs that have aged in wood at least four years, more with the better ones. Remy Martin VSOP, for instance, contains cognacs of six to eight years of age. Napoleon cognac is another step up, containing cognacs that are at least six years old, although generally much older, up to ten, eleven, or fifteen years in some cases. Several firms use proprietary names for cognacs of this level and older, such as Hennessy's Bras d'Or, Martell's Cordon Bleu, and Delamain's Vesper.

Further refinements have to do with the particular district of the Cognac region where the vineyards are located. Cognacs labeled Grande Champagne (*champagne* here has nothing to do with sparkling wine but is an old French word meaning "field") must come entirely from the top-rated district of that name. Fine Champagne may come only from the top two districts, 50 percent of it from Grande Champagne. The most exalted cognacs, such as Hine Triomphe, Remy's Louis XIII, or Hennessy's Paradis, contain the oldest and rarest cognacs, twenty-five to forty years old, often only from Grande Champagne.

Some of the most interesting cognacs are single-cask cognacs. They come from the top-rated vineyards of individual growers, usually only from the Grande Champagne district. Most cognacs are blended from many different casks of many different ages and several of the cognac districts; single-cask cognacs have a unique character of their own that comes from the particular soil of the vineyard as well as the aging process. Corti Brothers, a Sacramento grocery chain that offers many gourmet and delicacy items, imports a number of single-cask (and single-vintage) cognacs that can be found on the West Coast. Darrell Corti personally selects these brandies in France or in London and through the years has offered several "early-landed" cognacs from Hine and Frapin. Early-landed is an English term referring to young cognacs shipped to London in cask and aged there. Some of them are unusually refined in bouquet, with an intriguing complexity of flavor. Leading wine shops sometimes bring in special cognacs, and these are well worth trying.

ARMAGNAC

Armagnac, claimed to be the oldest French brandy, comes from Gascony, the land of d'Artagnan, also the land of truffles and foie gras. It does not have the lofty reputation of cognac, but it is by no means inferior to it. The climate of Gascony is warmer, its soil somewhat richer. Armagnac is aged in Gascon black oak (although some is aged in oak from the forests of Limousin), which gives it a different accent, a lustier warmth and flavor. Aging is again the determining factor in quality, a costly process that makes the older spirits more expensive. Designations similar to those of cognac are used—three-star, VSOP, X.O., or Extra. There are even vintage-dated armagnacs, although these are rare, as age is not permitted on brandies imported to the United States.

CALVADOS

Calvados is the apple brandy from Normandy, France. This winning spirit, with its alluring scent of fresh apples and fervent warmth, deserves to be better known in this country. The finest calvados comes from eastern Normandy, the region known as the Pays d'Auge, a verdant strip of fertile land that is home to apple orchards and dairy cows; in fact, they share the same turf. The local cows provide the milk for Normandy's famous cheeses—Camembert, Pont l'Évêque, and Livarot. The best cheeses also come from farms in the Pays d'Auge.

Fresh apples are pressed for calvados and the juice ferments slowly for a month before being distilled. Calvados from the Pays d'Auge is distilled in copper-pot stills in the same manner as cognac. The age of calvados is indicated as follows: three stars for two-year-old calvados; Vieux or Réserve is the designation for three-year-old; V.O. or Vieille Réserve is four years old; V.S.O.P. or Grand Réserve denotes five years; Extra, Napoleon, Hors d'Age, or Age *inconnu* are terms used for anything over five years old. Many such labels, however, contain much older brandies. Some Hors d'Age or Age *inconnu* calvados may be fifteen to twenty-five years old. Calvados produced outside the Pays d'Auge appellation is called *reglementé*. It does not have the complexity or finesse of Pays d'Auge, but it can still be quite good and is excellent for cooking and flambéing.

It would be difficult to choose which of the three brandies to keep on hand, since each has something in particular to recommend it. Cognac has the greatest finesse, the most ethereal and complex aroma. Armagnac, bolder and earthier than cognac, has ravishing warmth and richness of texture. Calvados is an excellent digestif, the one I often choose after a very big meal. In Normandy, tables are spread for trenchermen, and during one of the long Norman meals there is a pause in the middle for a shot of calvados. This fiery bolt is known as *le trou Normand,* or "the Norman hole," which is created by the spirit to make room for the rest of the meal. I usually keep all three of these amber spirits available, since I never know which one will suit the mood after dinner. It is nice to be able to offer guests a variety.

EAU-DE-VIE

The clear white fruit brandies, known as eaux-de-vie or *alcools blancs,* have a racy zest that makes them refreshing alternatives after dinner. They are a genuine challenge to the distiller's art— the slightest flaw or poor-quality fruit shows through. Because the quality of the fruit must be high, they are expensive to make. Framboise is made from raspberries, kirsch from cherries, mirabelle from yellow plums, poire from the Williams pear, fraise from strawberries, and quetsch from small purple plums. These are fruits that grow especially well in the Vosges Mountains of Alsace, France, the Black Forest region in southern Germany, and in parts of Austria and Switzerland.

It takes twenty to thirty kilos of raspberries to make a single bottle of framboise, which gives some idea as to why it is so expensive. Different firms are noted for a particular eau-de-vie, although they may produce a full line of a dozen or more. Massenez of Alsace, for instance, is noted for its framboise and mirabelle. The firm of Schladerer, situated in the Black Forest, makes excellent kirsch. Trimbach's most popular eau-de-vie is poire. Jean Danflou, a Paris-based brandy shipper noted for his astute palate, chooses some of the finest poire and framboise made to export under his label.

Eau-de-vie should be served cold, but not so cold as to numb the flavor or deaden the exhilarating fruit aroma for which these fruit brandies are prized. Some people like to keep them iced in the refrigerator, but others maintain that this ultimately robs them of flavor and fragrance. The late Jean Danflou had perhaps the best technique. At an impeccable little brandy boutique on Rue du Mont Thabor in Paris (near the Place Vendôme), visitors and prospective buyers could taste some of his wares. To serve poire or framboise, he simply swirled ice cubes in small stemmed snifters to chill the glasses, then poured in the eau-de-vie. This technique, he insisted, preserves the full intensity of the bouquet that makes them so special. Chilled eau-de-vie is an especially good choice for after dinner in summer, when other brandies might be too heavy.

GRAPPA

Finally, there is grappa, the Italian white brandy made from grape pomace, or in some cases the crushed grape and grape must, even occasionally from other fruits such as strawberries, cherries or raspberries. Many of the leading wine estates in Italy produce grappa— Ceretto, Gaja, Lungarotti, Querceto, Mastroberardino, Jermann, Monte Vertine and many others. The Nonino family of Friuli specialize in grappa, making a dozen or more from different grapes. The Noninos also pioneered the whole grape process for making grappa, which is known as UE (the term for "grape" in the Friulan dialect). Using such grapes as moscato, gewürztraminer, and the rare piccolit, the Noninos produce heady elixirs that sell for $80 to $100 or more per bottle. No serious Italian restaurant is without a roster of grappas, some quite extensive. Felidia Ristorante in Manhattan, for instance, stocks over forty grappas. Grappa, like eau-de-vie, is usually best chilled.

AMERICAN BRANDIES

In this country we have long had domestic spirits such as applejack, but during the eighties a few dedicated distillers sprang up. A relatively small group of artisans, they produce oak-aged brandy similar to cognac and eaux-de-vies that can rival some of the imports. Grappa and apple brandies are also produced. These spirits are well worth investigating as alternatives to imported ones. Some of the names to look for include Bonny Doon, Clear Creek, Creekside, Germain-Robin, Jepson and St. George.

Chapter 10

SERVING
AND STORING:
THE PRACTICAL
ASPECT

▼

*A house having a great wine stored below lives in our
imaginations as a joyful house, fast and splendidly rooted
in the soil.*

GEORGE MEREDITH, *The Egoist*

*T*he immediate enjoyment of wine requires nothing more than a bottle, a glass, and a corkscrew, suitable food, a "thou," if possible, or just a few chums. For grander wines and grander occasions, however, the proper accoutrements can add immeasurably to one's enjoyment. A table set with gleaming crystal is a beautiful sight and one that rouses anticipation for the evening ahead.

Glasses, decanters, corkscrews—there is sound reason for the evolution of the proper implement in each case.

Glassware

Size and shape are the two most important aspects to consider when choosing glasses. One good all-purpose glass will suffice, as long as it is large enough. Eight ounces is the minimum capacity, since the glass should never be more than half full (in order to swirl the wine and release the aroma). Ten- or twelve-ounce glasses are better, especially for red wines. Oversized glasses, those of more than sixteen ounces, are ungainly at best. They are so top-heavy when half filled with wine that it is awkward to hold them by the stem, much less swirl the wine with aplomb—in other words, without sloshing it over the rim.

Simple, unetched crystal is best for appreciating a wine's color and clarity. The glass should taper in at the rim to capture the aromatics as the wine opens up in contact with the air. It should have a smooth rim with no lip. This is purely for esthetic reasons: It simply feels better when you bring it to your lips. For this reason also, thin crystal is preferable and it is not just snob appeal or a myth that fine wine tastes better in fine crystal. You can experiment for yourself sometime by serving your friends the same wine blind in different glasses. The difference may be psychological as well as sensual, but it is no less valid for that.

There are two reasons why the proper way to hold a wineglass is by the stem. It prevents warming a chilled wine with the heat from your hand, and it keeps the glass unsullied with fingerprints and smudges so that you can appreciate the wine's color and appearance. A brandy snifter, by contrast, is designed for cupping in the palm specifically to warm the brandy naturally (rather than with the somewhat pretentious apparatus known as a brandy warmer), urging it gradually to unleash the aromas.

While the all-purpose glass can accommodate virtually any type of wine, including sparkling wine, it is nice to have glasses of assorted sizes, especially for dinner parties that involve a succession of wines. Glasses of different shapes prevent confusion between the wines, particularly if there are two or more wines of different types but the same color. Different glass shapes can also lend a note of elegance to the table. If you plan to compare two wines of the same type—two Chardonnays, for example, or Burgundies from different properties—you may want to use identical glasses, so that the wines have equal dimensions for aeration and will therefore develop under the same conditions.

If you want the closest to perfection in glassware—and can afford it—Riedel Crystal of Austria makes a full range of glasses specifically designed for certain types of wine. It may seem hard to believe that a Chardonnay tastes markedly better in the eleven-ounce glass Riedel has designed for it than in a Riesling or Bordeaux glass. Nevertheless, it does. Riedel has experimented scientifically to demonstrate that the shape and size of the bowl remarkably affect how the wine will strike the palate. For a high-acid wine like Riesling, the smaller tapered bowl accentuates the wine's fruit and lessens perception of acidity; in Chardonnay, which often tends to be low in acidity, the fuller shape enhances acidity and makes the wine seem more balanced. There are similar design distinctions on glasses used for Bordeaux and Burgundy. It is glass design based on maximum enjoyment of a wine's character and flavor. For a catalog of Riedel glassware, write to Riedel Crystal of America, Inc., 24 Aero Road, Bohemia, N.Y. 11716. Department stores in major cities also stock them.

There is a return of late to the use of antique glasses, many of which are graceful and beautiful. These are fine and even enhance the look of the wine, as long as they are not opaque or colored, or so densely etched that one cannot admire the color and brilliance of the wine, which are so major a part of its enjoyment. The principal types of glasses and their uses are:

ALL-PURPOSE The ten- to twelve-ounce taster's glass is the most

ALL-PURPOSE   BALLON

FLUTE

HOCK OR RHINE   SNIFTER   SHERRY OR PORT

versatile wineglass, and it can be used for any wine, red or white. Be sure that it cups inward at the rim to gather the aromas of the wine. Some glasses turn inward, then out again, which is acceptable if the flare is not too exaggerated.

FLUTE The Champagne flute, as the proper glass for bubbly is known, is tall and deep-set, so designed for maximum retention of the bubbles. There are two styles: those that curve inward like a crocus blossom, and those that taper outward like a royal trumpet. The shallow, saucer-shaped glass that used to be associated with Champagne should be avoided altogether because it dissipates the bubbles too quickly. Champagne glasses must be thoroughly rinsed and free of soap film or dust, which destroys the effervescence.

BALLON The wide bowl makes this glass ideal for Burgundy and other big red wines. There is more room for the aromas to expand and the rim curves inward slightly. Avoid glasses that are too large (more than sixteen ounces); they are awkward to handle.

HOCK OR RHINE A shallow bowl and long stem make this a graceful shape for such light white wines as Rieslings and Gewürztraminer.

SNIFTER The snifter for brandy can double as a glass for full-bodied red wines. It should be a minimum of eight ounces; many people prefer larger, twelve-ounce ones. Very large, bulbous glasses, however, are unnecessary and somewhat pretentious.

SHERRY OR PORT A port or sherry glass should hold at least two to three ounces. Port may also be served in small snifters, which help concentrate its aroma.

Decanters

Clear, crystal decanters show a wine's color and clarity to best advantage, although cut or etched crystal can be lovely if not too ornate or "busy." Decanters that are very thick and heavy can be cumbersome to handle. For simple aerating, glass carafes and ceramic pitchers are perfectly suitable. During my wine travels, I am always on the lookout for interesting pitchers to add to my collection of pouring vessels; I make good use of them for informal occasions.

The Rituals of Serving

A simple wine for a casual meal can simply be opened and poured without ceremony or fanfare (which would, in fact, be inappropriate). A certain ritual attends the serving of fine wines, but this must surely be accomplished in as relaxed a manner as the host can manage. The idea is not to make a fuss about the care that is taken or to call undue attention to things like opening the wine or decanting it: to do so is the height of pretentiousness and snobbery, and a crashing bore as well. Yet for wine lovers, a great deal of the pleasure of wine comes from the preparation that leads up to drinking it, the physical handling of the bottle—opening, decanting, pouring the wine itself.

Serving wine at the proper temperature is a critical factor in the enjoyment of it. Serving wine at the wrong temperature can ruin it or, at the very least, do it a grave disservice. A white wine can be too cold, or not cold enough; a red can be too warm. The style and type of wine have much to do with how the wine will come across.

WHITE WINES

Simple white wines and rosés may be chilled quite thoroughly, to 45 degrees or so. (Thermometers that measure wine temperature are available at shops that sell wine tools.) Fine white wines, however, should not be overchilled; the cold will numb their subtle flavors and complexity. In blind tastings or wine judgings the wines are often served at cool room temperature, about 65 degrees, but they are best for drinking somewhere between 50 and 55 degrees.

Chilling wine will take a good two hours in the refrigerator. It will go much faster in an ice bucket, which provides the quickest and most efficient way to cool wines. Just be sure to fill the bucket half with ice and the rest water, and the job will be done in twenty minutes or so. Ice by itself is useless; the bottle needs total submersion in cold. If the ice bucket is somewhat shallow, as most of them regrettably are, you may need to put the bottle in headfirst for the last few minutes to ensure that the wine is fully chilled. Always keep a cloth or napkin handy to wrap around the bottle when you remove it from the bucket so that you don't drip icy water on the table (or your guests).

Trying to chill a fine wine quickly in the freezer is not desirable either, although it is often done in an emergency. This drastic treatment can blunt the flavor and aroma. Nor is it advisable to chill fine white wines in the refrigerator too much in advance; they should be refrigerated no more than a few hours at most. Do not store fine whites at refrigerator temperatures for any length of time. This, too, can have a dulling effect on flavor and aroma.

RED WINES

If you have a cellar or a temperature-controlled storage system, red wines should be removed an hour or two before serving, so that they may warm up to about 65 or 68 degrees, which is just about ideal for most reds. The term *room temperature* is out-of-date today. It referred to the chillier rooms of yesteryear and not the 72-plus degrees of many present-day homes.

Wines purchased for dinner should be acquired at least a few days in advance and stored in a cool place to allow them to rest and settle after being moved about. Wines of ten years or more need much longer to rest after transport, up to a month or more, if possible.

Red wines that are eight to ten years old or older usually throw a deposit of sediment. This is quite natural and entirely harmless. It is even desirable in full-bodied reds, a sign that they are untampered with and originally had a certain amount of concentration and extract. Wines with sediment are best decanted (see pages 195–96); otherwise the action of pouring washes the sediment up into the glass. A muddy wine is not a pleasant sight and no one likes the taste of grit in the mouth.

THE BREATHING QUESTION

The amount of "breathing" time a wine should have is the single most controversial aspect of serving wine. A wine is said to "breathe" when in contact with the air; the various compounds (some four hundred of them have been isolated to date) meet with oxygen, and the interaction releases aromas and flavors. Traditionally, fine reds were opened an hour or two in advance of serving, depending on the wine's age and density. Pulling the cork, however, leaves nothing more than a two-inch space of air about the size of a penny, hardly enough to permit a useful exchange.

The precise moment at which a wine reaches fully developed flavor is difficult, if not impossible, to judge without recent experience with the wine involved. For that reason, many people (I among them) prefer to open a wine just before serving, decant, if necessary, and pour immediately, allowing it to breathe in the glass. The only problem here is that if you have a rather stiff, unyielding red, it may take quite a long time to loosen up, depriving you of full enjoyment until the last few sips. Such a wine requires patience, and it is typical of wines like Barolo, Brunello, or bigger Bordeaux like Château Latour or Mouton-Rothschild, or even the subtler Lafite. If you are aware of this, pull the cork thirty minutes to an hour ahead, but pour off a wineglass so that a greater volume of air can mix with the wine in the bottle.

Take care in opening or decanting older wines too soon. Very old ones may be extremely fragile and when in contact with air they may quickly lose their strength and flavor. This is another reason to open and decant just prior to serving.

DECANTING

There is nothing esoteric about decanting wine. I do it for most reds, even young ones with no sediment, just as a way of loosening them up a little sooner. Decanting to aerate a wine this way involves nothing more than pouring it into a carafe or pitcher, then pouring it back into the original bottle. Decanting a red wine or vintage port to remove sediment requires more care. You will need the following tools: a decanter, a corkscrew, a candle or some other light source, and a clean muslin cloth if it involves vintage port. You should then:

1. Remove the bottle from storage carefully so that you disturb the sediment as little as possible. Stand it upright about a day ahead so that the deposit will settle to the bottom of the bottle. Very old wines may rest in a cradle or basket instead of upright.

2. When you are ready to decant, or thirty minutes to an hour before serving, remove the cork, disturbing the wine as little as possible. I find the Screwpull best for this procedure, because it requires the least leverage and moves easily through the cork (see page 197). Wipe the rim of the bottle carefully with a clean cloth to remove mold, bits of cork, or dirt. Old port that is heavily encrusted with sediment may require pouring through muslin to filter it completely.

3. Hold the bottle so that the shoulder of the neck is directly over the candle (or electric light or upended flashlight), and pour evenly without interruption until a dark line of sediment appears in the neck. Stop pouring immediately. The wine in the decanter should be bright and clear, with only an inch or so of gritty wine remaining in the bottle.

The thoughtful host will place the bottle within sight so that guests can see the label—unless, of course, the group indulges in tasting blind. This is a jolly parlor game among wine buffs, an irresistible challenge that can be fun if undertaken in the right spirit and in like-minded company. It is not done, however, unless it is something that all those present would enjoy. If your guests are not familiar with such games, if they would feel put on the spot or in any way embarrassed by them, then forget it.

White wines benefit by contact with the air just as red wines do, although generally it is not necessary to decant them. White wines occasionally throw a harmless sediment of tartrate crystals.

Tartrates are a natural constituent of wine, but their presence alarms some people because the crystals look like grains of sugar or shards of glass. Sometimes they cling to the cork or wash up when the wine is poured, but they are entirely harmless and do not affect the taste of the wine.

CORKSCREWS

There are many styles of corkscrews, as illustrated here. In terms of efficiency, the most important factors are leverage and the construction of the bore, or worm. The wingtip, the double action, and the screwpull provide the best leverage, especially for women. The waiter's friend works very well for those who have mastered it but requires an understanding of its unique leverage; the old T-bar and the Ah-So work well as long as the cork is not stubborn. Although I have versions of all types, the one I invariably use is the Leverpull, an advanced model of Screwpull. It works best with a minimum of effort on all sorts of corks, including old fragile ones or tight new ones. The pocket model, called pocketpull, is especially handy for traveling.

Ideally, the worm of the corkscrew should be a perfect helix, a true open spiral with rounded edges about two inches in length. Many of the cheaper corkscrews have sharp edges, which can tear a cork to pieces and never get it out. A worm that is too short will not penetrate the longer corks of better wines.

OPENING THE BOTTLE

Opening a wine bottle gets easier with practice, but these are steps that facilitate the procedure.

1. Using a sharp blade, cut around the capsule a quarter-inch or so below the rim of the bottle. The wine should not come in contact with the lead foil (or plastic) of the capsule, which can affect the taste.

2. Wipe mold or dirt from the cork top with a clean cloth.

3. Remove the cork. Wipe away any remaining residue of mold, dirt, or bits of cork.

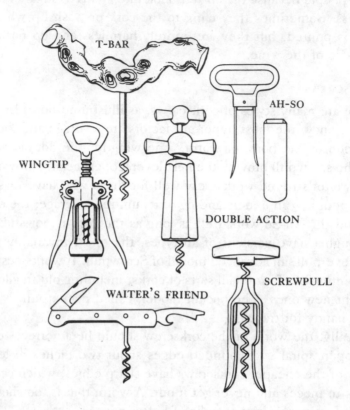

T-BAR

AH-SO

WINGTIP

DOUBLE ACTION

WAITER'S FRIEND

SCREWPULL

Opening Champagne and Sparkling Wines

Champagne corks are wired on so the cork won't fly off prematurely from the tremendous pressure inside the bottle. Handle Champagne bottles gently so as not to make a lethal missile out of the cork. Do not let it pop out violently; not only is this dangerous but it wastes the wine and will dissipate the bubbles sooner.

1. Remove the foil to a point just below the base of the wire; some foils have a perforated guide around the rim.

2. Hold the bottle at roughly a 45-degree angle, pointing it away from yourself and anybody else.

3. Remove the wire and hold the crown of the cork with one hand. Twist the bottle with the other hand to loosen the cork. When you feel the cork start to yield, hold it in place and gently ease it out. Have a flute glass handy in case the wine rushes forth.

4. If the cork is too stubborn to remove by hand, a pair of Champagne pliers is useful to give it a nudge. Use the pliers just to loosen the cork. As soon as it gives slightly, set the pliers aside and gently twist it out the rest of the way.

5. If the top of the cork breaks off you may use a corkscrew to remove it, but be very careful to position the bottle so that the pressurized cork does not fly out with the corkscrew attached, injuring you or someone else.

Champagne stoppers are an excellent way to keep the bubbles flowing if you have leftover wine. Sparkling wine will keep in good condition for at least a few days in the refrigerator when tightly stoppered.

Some of the rituals that evolved in serving wine were originally grounded in good sense. Smelling the cork, for example, offers the first opportunity to check the soundness of the wine. The end that was in contact with the wine should smell of wine, not of cork. If it smells of cork, the wine itself may be "corked," which is the winetaster's term for a wine that has a corky smell rather than a winy one.

The cork must be smelled the instant it is withdrawn; otherwise it is useless because the aroma of the wine evaporates almost immediately. Thus, the waiter's gesture of handing you the cork to smell in a restaurant is a meaningless one, other than to confirm that it is stamped with proper identification of property and/or vintage. I am in the habit of glancing at the cork for that reason, and it is a good idea to do so.

Just as the host customarily tastes the wine at a restaurant before it is poured to be sure it is all right, the host at home should pour a little of the wine into his glass first. This is merely a courtesy, for the most part, to collect any bits of cork that may issue from the first pouring, but it also gives the host a chance to check a newly opened bottle to be sure it is sound. This is, of course, unnecessary if the wine has been checked earlier when opened for aeration or decanting.

Glasses should be filled only halfway or slightly less, leaving room to swirl the wine and aerate it further. This also allows space for the aromas of the wine to collect. For many wine lovers, aroma offers as much pleasure as the actual taste of a wine.

It is irritating to have wine sloppily poured, dribbling it down the side of the glass to drip in your lap as you drink. Some people use a napkin to catch the dribbles, but with a little practice you can master the art of pouring without spills. When you've finished pouring, give the bottle a slight turn as you tilt it upward—still over the glass—to conquer the drips. Remember to use a cloth or napkin for chilled wines that may be slippery or for wines taken from the ice bucket.

Buying and Storing

Wine-buying habits have changed considerably in the last decade. Most consumers have discovered the convenience of keeping a quantity of wine on hand to draw on as needed. It is a nuisance to have to run out and buy a bottle each time you plan to serve wine, but there are several other advantages to acquiring wine by the case.

There are two main reasons for establishing a wine cellar—or the modern equivalent of one. One is the convenience it affords; the other is to enable you to purchase fine wines when they come on the market and age them for future enjoyment. An advantage of buying ahead is that it allows you to obtain wines that might be scarce or unavailable at a later date, or offered only at inflated prices if they are available at all. Furthermore, with your own wine cellar, you can be sure of the storage conditions under which the wines have matured.

Buying ahead also allows you to plan, to consider the types of wine that you will need, as well as to take advantage of specials that are offered. Wine lovers get enormous pleasure in collecting wines, keeping track of what they have, what they need to replenish, or new vintages that they want to stock. It is an absorbing hobby, but it can get out of hand rather suddenly for those who lose track of what they have and fail to drink up wines that have reached the peak of readiness.

PHILOSOPHY OF A CELLAR

The concept of the wine cellar is rapidly changing to meet the needs of today. No longer does the term refer solely to an underground storage area. Today the term *cellar* is used in a broader sense to designate any system for storing wine. For apartment dwellers, it may be a closet, a cache of racks in the living room, or a custom-designed, temperature-controlled cabinet.

Cellars of yore were ideal for storing wines that needed several years of aging. The atmosphere was cool, humid, insulated against fluctuations in temperature, stable, quiet, and dark so that the wines could lie undisturbed and protected from harmful light. The closer one can come to such conditions for storing wine, the better. Modern basements that house the washer, the dryer, and the furnace may not be the most desirable place for storing wines, unless there is a room or a corner well away from such units.

Following are the most important factors to consider in setting up a wine cellar.

TEMPERATURE Select the coolest place available, avoiding areas near heating units or air conditioners that would subject the wine to dramatic fluctuations in temperature. Wine matures more slowly and evenly at cooler temperatures, ideally between 53 and 57 degrees, but it will do reasonably well in an atmosphere of 68 or 70 degrees as long as the temperature is fairly constant.

HUMIDITY A humidity level of 60 to 70 percent is ideal for storing wine. If the atmosphere is too humid, the labels will disintegrate and mold or fungus can develop too readily. Some will have no objection to such condition; certainly it lends a special atmosphere to the aged cellars of Europe. The situation is far worse if the atmosphere is too dry; the cork may dry up even though the wines are stored on their sides. A humidifier (or, if it is too humid, a dehumidifier) can help, and a container of damp sand will promote humidity in smaller storage areas.

VIBRATION Wine should not be stored in heavily trafficked areas like hallways, or near machines that vibrate (like refrigerators or air conditioners). Constant or even intermittent vibration keeps a wine unsettled and in older wines may disturb sediment. Keep wine in a quiet, stable area free from vibration.

LIGHT Direct light, whether natural or artificial, is harmful to wine and may alter its chemistry, which is why most wines intended for aging are bottled in dark green or brown bottles. Wines in clear bottles are particularly vulnerable. Fluorescent light, except for full-spectrum types such as Vitalite, is especially harmful to wine.

STOCKING THE HOME CELLAR

Fine wines that need several years of bottle age demand ideal storage conditions. There is no point in paying high sums for expensive wines if you cannot provide space with optimum temperature control at a minimum of 55 to 60 degrees. Under reasonable conditions, however, it is still possible to stock a goodly store of wine for current drinking or for enjoying over the next few years.

In getting started, think in terms of a two-tiered cellar. The first tier, so to speak, would include wines for immediate drinking, casual wines for everyday use as well as better wines for entertaining that are ready to drink. The second tier would include wines that require time to mature. This part of your cellar could be further subdivided with wines that will be ready within a year or two, wines that need two or three years of aging, and wines that need five or six.

At first, the two tiers may be evenly divided so that you have a sufficient number of wines to draw on while the others age. If you begin, say, with four or six cases, at least half should be wines that you can open and drink as soon as you like. Note the wines from the lighter categories in the "Table of Wine Styles" (page 221). These can be replenished as needed. The other half of the cellar is one you may want to expand as space permits and as new wines worth cellaring become available.

The following are suggested categories of wines to consider for the two-tiered cellar. Try to start with at least two mixed cases, adding to them according to the space you have and what you can afford to spend. The range of prices listed is approximate. Buying by the case may include a 10 percent discount. In terms of vintages, it is best to consult a recent vintage chart or discuss with your wine merchant the differences in available vintage years.

LIGHT WINES AND ROSÉS
Price range: $5 to $10 per bottle
Chenin Blanc, Riesling, Gewürztraminer, Muscadet, Mâcon Blanc, Sancerre, Italian Chardonnay, Pinot Gris, Pinot Bianco, Pinot Grigio, Pinot Blanc, Sauvignon Blanc (or Fumé Blanc), Sablet Blanc, Vouvray, dry or off-dry rosés such as Tavel, Cabernet d'Anjou, blush wines, *vin gris*, Castel del Monte, Chiaretto, Zinfandel, or Grenache.

These are wines to drink within three to six months of purchase or they will lose much of their freshness and charm. Many of them make suitable aperitifs.

LIGHT REDS
Price range: $5 to $12 per bottle
Beaujolais-Villages and village or *cru* Beaujolais (Brouilly, Fleurie, Morgon, Chénas, Chiroubles, Juliénas, Saint-Amour, Moulin-à-Vent), Gamay Beaujolais, Cabernet del Friuli, Italian Merlot, Côtes du Rhône, Côtes du Ventoux, Lirac, Côtes du Roussillon, simple Chianti, Rioja, Dolcetto d'Alba, Barbera, Valtellina reds, Zinfandel.

WEIGHTIER WHITES
Price range: $10 to $30, and up
White Graves (château-bottled), Chardonnay, French Chablis,

white Burgundy (Meursault, Puligny-Montrachet, Chassagne-Montrachet, Corton-Charlemagne, the *grand cru* Montrachets), white Hermitage, Viognier, Marsanne/Roussanne, German *Kabinett* and *Spätlese* Riesling.

MEDIUM REDS

Price range: $10 to $20, and up
Cru bourgeois Bordeaux from lesser châteaux, such as Gloria, Greysac, La Tour de By, Fourcas-Hosten, Senéjac, Larose-Trintaudon, and numerous others; Chianti Riserva, Rioja Riserva, moderate-priced California Cabernets and Zinfandels; Oregon Pinot Noir, Rhône Valley reds such as Gigondas, Saint-Joseph, Crozes-Hermitage, Châteauneuf-du-Pape, California Rhône blends.

WEIGHTIER REDS

Price range: $16 to $35, higher for top growths and reserve wines
Classified Bordeaux from the Médoc, Pomerol, Saint-Émilion, and Graves; red Burgundy, California Cabernet Sauvignon, California Merlot, California Syrah and Petite Sirah. Reserves and proprietary blends (Opus One, Le Clos, Rubicon, Lyeth, Carmenet, Meritage), Hermitage, Côte Rôtie, Cornas, Barolo, Barbaresco, Brunello di Montalcino, Sassicaia, Tignanello, and other *vino da tavola*, Taurasi, Pesquera, Ribera del Duero, Gran Coronas.

DESSERT AND SPARKLING

Price range: variable
Champagne and/or other sparkling wines, Sauternes, *Auslese* Riesling, late-harvest Riesling or Gewürztraminer, dessert Muscats, ruby or tawny port, vintage port.

KEEPING A CELLAR BOOK

In order for a cellar to be workable and convenient, it has to be replenished as you draw from it. Even though your cellar may be a small one at first, it is advisable to keep a log of the inventory, perhaps make a diagram of the various bins and what they hold. When a bin is down to half its stock, it is time to replenish, but not necessarily with the same wines. As is particularly the case among the lighter ones, other wines may have come along that are fresher or of better value.

Cellar books outlined for keeping track of individual wines are available in many sizes and formats, but a spiral or looseleaf notebook can serve if you organize it properly. Create categories that take note of when you bought the wine and for how much, when you drank it, and brief notes about its quality or progress. If possible, give some indication of the quantity remaining. Use it to browse through when planning new purchases or just to recall pleasurable occasions. It will not be of much use, however, unless you keep it fairly up-to-date.

Chapter 11

TASTING:
A SENSUAL
APPROACH

▼

Good wine, well drunk, can lend majesty to the human spirit. The rules are simple, and if followed will add pleasure to the simplest palate, the simplest meal, and make it grow.

M. F. K. FISHER, *The Story of California Wine*

*I*t is often said that "a little learning is a dangerous thing." This adage certainly rings true with wine. We have all met with wine snobs or pedants who take every opportunity to show off, babbling arcane facts of wine jargon that have no place at a social occasion, even one designed principally around fine bottles. These meager personalities are to be shunned at all costs.

It is true, however, that when a group involved professionally with wine get together, the conversation often revolves around little else. I enjoy this sort of ingrown preoccupation if it does not take place too often, but I would never subject other friends to it (or risk boring them to tears with it) unless I knew for certain they would get a kick out of it.

The fact remains that some knowledge of wine, no matter how little, greatly increases the enjoyment of it. As with most of life's pleasures, knowing something of what to expect creates anticipation of the experience. I can personally vouch for the fact that as you come to know more about wine, you will accumulate more than just a store of knowledge on that subject alone. This becomes clear as you try different wines, acquaint yourself with a broader range of styles, and begin to discover your own likes and dislikes.

There is only one way to learn about wine and that is by tasting it. Drinking wine occasionally or frequently, you absorb a certain understanding, if only by osmosis and repetition. The most methodical and specific way to learn more is to organize tastings with a few friends and set to it. I believe people take wine classes more for the organized tastings involved than for any other reason. Many wine enthusiasts are also forming small tasting groups that get together once or twice a month just to explore a few wines.

A wine tasting is not difficult to organize, and it is fun as well as instructive. It can be done on a weekend afternoon, followed simply by cheese and bread; or it can take place before an informal supper or dinner. The following are some of the things to keep in mind for setting up a wine tasting.

CHOOSING THE WINES

One learns most by comparing wines of the same type, all Bordeaux, or Chardonnays, or Rheingau Rieslings. Take six or eight Bordeaux, for example, all of the same vintage, and you should come away with a useful sense of what Bordeaux is like, how it can vary in style and depth, which style you prefer. You can select a broader range of wines if you prefer, one that includes wines from different regions, or different parts of the same region—several whites from the Loire Valley, for instance, to help you distinguish between Muscadet and Pouilly-Fumé. If the range is too broad, however, if you include, say, a Bordeaux, a Barolo, a Chianti, and a Zinfandel in a single tasting, all it would show is how dramatically different the wines are from one another. A single wine may not be especially representative of its type. How much more useful to taste six Zinfandels; then you have some idea of what to expect the next time you buy one.

A Champagne tasting is great fun, and an excellent way to discover the best values in sparkling wine around the holidays. If you are trying to decide which one to buy, arrange a tasting and suggest that each person bring a different bottle. This can be a most instructive tasting, but I must warn you, it can get very merry very quickly indeed.

EQUIPMENT

Use a table large enough to give reasonable space between bottles so that people do not bunch into one spot to pour the wine. The surface of the tasting table should be white so that the tasters can observe the color of the wine. A paper tablecloth is fine and you do not have to worry about stains. Failing that, have a sheet of white paper at each taster's place for him or her to judge the wine against.

Glasses should be at least eight ounces in size. Have at least two per person in case people want to directly compare two wines. Ideally, if one has six wines, there should be six glasses for each taster. That can mean a lot of glasses if you have six or more tasters. One solution is to rent wineglasses, which includes the added advantage of having glasses of all the same size. I do not advise using plastic glasses at a wine tasting. You cannot get a true impression of the wine because plastic has a certain smell of its own; sometimes you can taste it as well. Nor are most plastic glasses the proper size or shape.

Have a separate table for pitchers of water, extra glasses, bread or crackers, and napkins.

Some tasters prefer not to swallow the wine at a tasting, particularly if several (more than six) wines are included. Spitting buckets are therefore essential, though some people may choose not to use them. It can be any sort of vessel, from a real brass spittoon to a ceramic pitcher to a pasteboard paint container to individual paper cups. I use a red fire bucket, with an inch of slightly soapy water in the bottom to make for easy cleaning. A box filled with sand or sawdust would be even better. Some people are revolted by the idea of spitting, but if you are tasting a number of wines (particularly Champagne, which goes to your head like a rocket), the impressions can get fairly blurred after a while. If you taste a wine properly, you should be able to get a clear impression of it without swallowing; all it takes is a little practice.

Serving the Wines

Collect the wines several days in advance, if you can, so that they have time to rest and settle down. Chill the white wines about two hours ahead and open them at the last minute. I generally open red wines just before the tasting as well (unless they are vintage ports, which should be opened and decanted a few hours in advance) and let them do their breathing in the glass. Arrange the wines in a tasting order that leads from the lightest to the heaviest, provided there is such a progression. If the tasting involves a small group, some people make it a sit-down party. At such a party have the glasses set before each place in manageable order—in an arc if there are only a few wines, in several rows if there are more than six or eight. Be sure each person has a napkin and an extra glass for water.

Make a list of the wines available, noting the name, appellation of origin, vintage, and price. (If the tasting is blind, hand the list out later.) It is also helpful to have pencil and paper handy for people to take notes.

Pour out two to four ounces of each wine, no more, so that there is plenty of room in the glass for swirling to aerate the wine.

Tasting Blind

Many people prefer to taste "blind"—that is, with the labels covered so that no one knows which wine is which. Remove the entire capsule that covers the cork; then wrap the bottles in brown bags and secure them with rubber bands or tape. White wines will keep a chill better if wrapped in foil. Be sure the wrapping clears the lip of the bottle so that when it is poured the wine does not come in contact with paper or aluminum foil, which might affect the taste. It is also important to number each bottle; this is an easy way for the tasters to keep track of the wines until the labels are unveiled.

Clearing the Palate

Slices of French bread or unsalted crackers are best served during the tasting. These foods are as important for quelling stirred-up gastric juices as for clearing the palate. You may include mild cheeses, if you like, but it may be better to bring out cheese, fruit, and other snacks after the tasting so that nothing interferes with the taste of the wine.

Whether your tasting is purely social in nature or more serious, remember that it is always informative to taste several wines against one another. Some guests may be more into it than others, but exchanging impressions can be very enlightening. Everybody should be encouraged to note the various elements of aroma and flavor for each wine. The more personal you are in recording impressions (tastes that remind you of mint, or raspberries or peaches, or rubber tires) the more likely you are to remember the wine. If it is a blind tasting, wait until everyone has finished sampling before you begin discussing the wines.

The Proper Steps

Tasting a wine to evaluate its quality is a little more involved than merely drinking, but anybody can do it. Basically, it is just a matter of paying attention to what is in your glass. The amount of attention required depends on the wine. One tosses back a simple Beaujolais or Zinfandel without much thought other than to note its charming fruit. Even these, however, deserve fuller assessment at a wine tasting. There are whole books on the art of tasting wine, the best being Michael Broadbent's *Guide to Wine Tasting;* it is the last word on the subject, but here, briefly, are a few notes.

Tasting involves all the senses. The first one for me is smell. As soon as a wine is poured, I give it a swirl and a sniff, looking for the first clues to its quality. Is it clean, does it have a fruity, winy aroma? Or is it smothered in sulphur fumes (sulphur dioxide is a preservative used in all winemaking, although less today than formerly) or other off-odors? Does it speak of its type—herbaceous like Sauvignon Blanc, or spicy like Gewürztraminer? You do not have to ask these questions specifically. As you get used to tasting, the aromas themselves suggest them.

After I have checked the aroma of the wine—a subject I will return to later—I look at its color and clarity. Color says a great deal about a wine. Young reds, for instance, show vibrant red or purplish hues; very old ones may be fading, but mature reds should still be vibrant, although darker in color and beginning to lighten just at the edges. White wines also take on a deeper color as they age, becoming more golden, losing some of the green highlights that were there in youth. Any hint of brown or amber in a wine, whether red or white, is a sign of oxidation, or maderization. *Maderisé*, as the French call it, is a term derived from *Madeira*. A maderized wine often has an aroma reminiscent of Madeira or sherry. The wine may still be quite drinkable, however; some people even like a touch of oxidized flavor.

After examining the color, I smell again. The wine will undoubtedly have changed for better or worse. As it airs, it opens up to reveal more of what it really is, but this may take a while. I remember a dinner in California at the home of a winemaker that proved this point very well. Conversation at one point turned on the different styles of Bordeaux and Cabernet Sauvignon. We were drinking Cabernet and the winemaker left the table and returned in a few minutes with a bottle of 1964 Château Latour from his cellar. He allowed as how this was not the best treatment for such an illustrious bottle, but we were all eager to taste it. When he poured it out, we all sniffed and wrinkled our noses at the off-odors, then set it aside to air a bit. Ten or fifteen minutes later the stale, acrid aromas persisted and some began to think it was an off-bottle. Another quarter-hour passed and someone suddenly said, "Hey, get a whiff of that Latour now!" The effluvia that had hung about it had lifted like fog. The wine, one of the best from the 1964 vintage, began to emerge in full glory; it just took its own sweet time doing so.

Finally, I taste, making note of the wine's texture, its body. Is it light and delicate, or rich and viscous, smooth or harsh? Does it have a long, pleasant aftertaste, or is it flat in finish? At a wine tasting, the thorough assessment of a wine at this point involves rolling it around in your mouth, "chewing" it, in a sense, and at the same time drawing in a small amount of air (not much, or you will choke) that mixes with the wine and releases all the flavor. *Do not* do this at a dinner table, unless you are in the company of those who would not consider it rude, vulgar, or simply odd behavior. By all means, however, give the wine the fullest attention you can. Enjoy its color, take in the bouquet of aromas, let it roll around in your mouth, but do so discreetly and without calling attention to yourself.

You may wonder where the sense of hearing comes in, and it is not overtly involved in the examination of wine. Sensually speaking, sound has more to do with the esthetics of the experience and is incidental, like an afterthought or a theatrical aside—the delicious gurgle of the wine as it is poured, the clink of glasses in a toast, something as delicate as the "murmuring froth" that Colette called Champagne or as raucous as the rising decibel in a room of happy topers.

A Wine Taster's Glossary

Acetic. Vinegary taste or smell that develops when a wine is overexposed to air.

Acidity. All wines naturally contain acids, which should be in proper balance with fruit and other components. Sufficient acidity gives liveliness and crispness and is critical for wines to age.

Aftertaste. The flavor impression the wine leaves after it is swallowed. Fine wines have a lingering aftertaste.

Aroma. The smell of a wine, especially a young wine.

Aromatic. A term for wines with pronounced aroma, particularly those redolent of herbs or spices.

Astringent. The puckerish quality of high tannin content, which has the effect of drying out the mouth. Many young red wines are astringent because of tannin.

Austere. Somewhat hard, with restrained fruit and character.

Balance. Harmony among the wine's components—fruit, acidity, tannins, alcohol; a well-balanced wine possesses the various elements in proper proportion to one another.

Big. Powerful in aroma and flavor; full-bodied.

Bitter. Usually considered a fault in wine but characteristic of such wines as Amarone and certain other Italian reds.

Body. The weight and texture of a wine; it may be light-bodied or full-bodied. Often refers to alcohol content.

Botrytis. A mold that attacks certain grapes, producing honeyed sweet wines like Sauternes and late-harvest Rieslings.

Bouquet. The complex of aromas that develops with age in fine wines; young wines have aroma, not bouquet.

Breed. Similar to good bloodlines and handling, as in racehorses; the result of soil, grapes, and vinification techniques that combine to produce distinctive character.

Buttery. Rich flavor and smoothness of texture somewhat akin to butter. More often refers to white wines than reds; many Chardonnays and white Burgundies are said to have buttery aroma and flavor.

Clean. Fresh, with no discernible defects; refers to aroma, appearance, and flavor.

Closed. Young, undeveloped wines that do not readily reveal their character are said to be closed. Typical of young Bordeaux or Cabernet Sauvignon, as well as other big red wines.

Coarse. Rude or harsh in flavor; clumsy or crude.

Complete. Mature, with good follow-through on the palate, satisfying mouth-feel, and firm aftertaste.

Complex. Multifaceted aroma or flavor. Complexity is essential for a wine to be considered great.

Cooked. Heavy, pruney flavor; also said of wines from very hot growing regions or wines that are overripe.

Corked, Corky. Smelling of cork rather than wine; due to a faulty cork.

Crisp. Fresh, brisk character, usually with high acidity.

Deep. Having layers of persistent flavor that gradually unfold with aeration.

Delicate. Light fragrance, flavor, and body.

Developed. Mature. A well-developed wine is more drinkable than an undeveloped one.

Distinctive. Elegant, refined character that sets the wine apart on its own.

Dry. Opposite of sweet.

Dull. Lacking liveliness and proper acidity; uninteresting.

Dumb. Not revealing flavor or aroma; typical of wines that are too young or too cold.

Earthy. Smell or flavor reminiscent of earth. A certain earthiness can be appealing; too much makes the wine coarse.

Elegant. Refined character, distinguished quality, stylish, not heavy.

Fat. Full of body and flavor; fleshy.

Fine. Distinguished.

Finesse. Distinctive balance; fineness; elegance and flair.

Finish. Aftertaste, or final impression the wine leaves; it can have a long finish or a short one (not desirable).

Firm. Taut balance of elements; tightly knit structure; also distinct flavor.

Flat. Dull, lacking grip or firmness.

Flavor. How the wine tastes.

Fleshy. Fatness of fruit; big, ripe.

Flinty. Dry, mineral character that comes from certain soils in which the wine was grown; typical of Chablis and some Sauvignon Blancs.

Flowery. Aroma suggestive of flowers.

Forward. Developed ahead of its peers; also, when the fruit is prominent, it is said to be forward.

Foxy. The "grapey" flavors of wines made from native American grapes, *Vitis labrusca*.

Fresh. Youthful, clean, vibrant, lively.

Fruity. Aroma and/or flavor of grapes; most common to young, light wines, but refers also to such fruit flavors in wine as apple, black currant, cherry, citrus, pear, peach, raspberry, or strawberry; descriptive of wines in which the fruit is dominant.

Full-bodied. Full proportion of flavor and alcohol; fat.

Grip. Firmness of flavor and structure.

Hard. Stiff, with pronounced tannins; undeveloped.

Harmonious. All elements in perfect balance.

Harsh. Rough, biting character from excessive tannin or acid.

Heady. High in alcohol, very full-bodied.

Herbaceous. Aromas and flavors reminiscent of grass or hay; grassy.

Herby. Reminiscent of herbs, such as mint, sage, thyme, or of eucalyptus.

Honest. Without flaws, typical and straightforward, decent but not great.

Honeyed. Smell or taste reminiscent of honey, characteristic of late-harvest wines affected by "noble rot" (*Botrytis cinerea*).

Intricate. Interweaving of subtle complexities of aroma and flavor.

Legs. The viscous rivulets that run down the side of the glass after swirling or sipping, a mingling of glycerine and alcohol.

Length. Lingering aftertaste.

Light. Refers usually to wines light in alcohol but also refers to texture and weight, how the wine feels in the mouth. Lightness is appropriate in some wines, a defect in others.

Lively. Crisp, fresh, having vitality.

Long. Fine wines should have a long finish, or aftertaste; see also *Length*.

Luscious. Rich, opulent, and smooth; most often said of sweet wines.

Maderized. Wine that has oxidized; has brown or amber color and stale odor.

Mature. Fully developed, ready to drink.

Meaty. A wine with chewy, fleshy fruit; sturdy and firm in structure.

Mellow. Smooth and soft, with no harshness.

Moldy. Wines with the smell of mold or rot, usually from grapes affected by rot or from old moldy casks used for aging.

Muscular. Vigorous fruit, powerful body and flavor; robust.

Musty. Stale, dusty aromas.

Noble. Great; of perfect balance and harmonious expression.

Nose. The smell of the wine; it may have a "good nose" or an "off-nose," meaning defective odors.

Nutty. Nutlike aromas that develop in certain wines, such as sherries or old whites.

Oak. Aroma and flavor that derive from aging in oak casks or barrels. Should not be overly pronounced.

Off-dry. Not quite dry, a perception of sweetness too faint to call the wine sweet.

Off-flavors (also *off-aromas* or *off-nose*). Not quite right; flavors or odors that are not correct for a particular type of wine; opposite of clean; defective.

Open. Revealing full character.

Oxidized. Flat, stale aroma and flavor; spoiled as the result of overexposure to air.

Pétillant. A light sparkle.

Rich. Full, opulent flavor, body, and aroma.

Ripe. Mature, fully ripe fruit.

Robust. Full-bodied, powerful, heady.

Rough. Harsh edges, biting, unpleasant.

Round. Smooth and well-developed flavor; usually medium- to full-bodied.

Sharp. Biting acid or tannin.

Short. Refers to finish, or aftertaste, when it ends abruptly.

Silky. Smooth, sinuous texture and finish.

Simple. Opposite of complex; straightforward.

Smoky. Aroma and flavor sometimes associated with wood.

Soft. May refer to soft, gentle fruit in delicate wines, or to flabbiness or lack of acidity in wines without proper structure.

Solid. Sound, well structured, firm.

Sour. Sharply acidic or vinegary.

Sparkling. Wines with bubbles created by trapped carbon dioxide gas, either natural or injected.

Spicy. Having the character or aroma of spices such as clove, mint, cinnamon, or pepper.

Spritzy. Slight prickle of carbon dioxide, common to some very young wines.

Steely. Firmly structured; taut balance tending toward high acidity.

Stiff. Unyielding; dumb.

Strong. Robust, powerful, big.

Structure. The way a wine is built; its composition.

Stuffing. Big, flavorful, full-bodied wines are said to have "stuffing."

Sturdy. Bold, vigorous flavor; full-bodied; robust.

Sulphur, SO₂. Scent of burned matches due to sulphur dioxide, an antioxidant used in making most wines.

Supple. Yielding in flavor; accessible and giving.

Tannin. A natural component found to varying degrees in the skins, seeds, and stems of grapes; most prominent in red wines, where it creates a dry, puckering sensation in young reds of concentrated extract; mellows with aging and drops out of the wine to form sediment; a major component in the structure of red wines.

Tart. Sharp; acceptable if not too acidic.

Thick. Dense and heavy.

Thin. Lacking body and flavor.

Tired. Past its peak of flavor development; old.

Tough. Astringent or hard.

Vanilla. A scent imparted by aging in oak.

Velvety. Smooth and rich in texture.

Vigorous. Firm, lively fruit, strong body; assertive flavor.

Vinegary. Having the smell of vinegar; see also *Acetic.*

Watery. Thin, lacking in flavor and color.

Weak. Lacking grip typical for the wine; without character.

Weedy. Aromas or flavors reminiscent of hay or grasses; not necessarily unpleasant unless exaggerated.

Weighty. Strong, powerful, full-bodied.

Woody. Excessive aromas of wood, common to wines aged overlong in cask.

Yeasty. A bready smell, characteristic of wines that have undergone a secondary fermentation, notably Champagne.

Young. In simple wines, signifies youthful freshness; in finer wines, refers to immaturity, wines as yet undeveloped.

A Table of
Wine Styles

Many of the wines mentioned in this book are referred to in terms of style, such as light and fruity, or rich and full-bodied. The table below lists wines by such categories as a quick reference, and suggests appropriate foods to serve with them. Note that there are a few overlaps. Inexpensive Italian or other Chardonnays, for example, are dry and light-bodied; other Chardonnays are rich and complex.

WHITE WINES	
	COMPATIBLE FOODS

DRY, LIGHT-BODIED

Beaujolais Blanc	Trout and other light fish, pasta,
Chardonnay	chicken salad, mild cheese,
Côtes du Rhône Blanc	vegetable crêpes
Fendant	
Frascati	
Galestro	
Grüner Veltliner	
Lugana	
Mâcon-Villages	
Mâcon-Viré	

DRY, LIGHT-BODIED

Muscadet	Trout and other light fish,
Orvieto	pasta, chicken salad, mild
Pinot Bianco	cheese, vegetable crêpes
Pinot Grigio	
Riesling (*Kabinett*)	
Rioja Blanco	
Seyval Blanc	
Soave	
Trebbiano	
Verdicchio	
Vernaccia di San Gimignano	
Vidal Blanc	
Vinho Verde	
Vouvray *sec*	

DRY, MEDIUM-BODIED

Aligoté	Fish and shellfish, poultry, light
Fiano di Avellino	meats, pâtés, goat cheese
Fumé Blanc	
Gavi	
Graves (white)	
Marsanne/Roussanne	
Pinot Blanc	
Pinot Gris	
Pouilly-Fuissé	
Pouilly-Fumé	
Riesling (Alsace)	
Saint-Véran	
Sancerre	
Seyval Blanc	
Sylvaner (Alsace)	
Tokay d'Alsace	

OFF-DRY (A TOUCH OF SWEETNESS)

California Chablis
Chenin Blanc
French Colombard
Gewürztraminer
Orvieto *abboccato*
Riesling
Sylvaner
Vouvray *demi-sec*

Aperitifs, Oriental food, poultry and light meats, fruit, mild cheeses

FULL-BODIED, COMPLEX FLAVOR (DRY)

Chablis (French)
Chardonnay
Chassagne-Montrachet
Condrieu
Corton-Charlemagne
Gewürztraminer (Alsace)
Greco di Tufo
Hermitage Blanc
Meursault
Montrachet
Puligny-Montrachet
Savennières
Viognier

Fish, chicken, or veal in rich sauces

SWEET WHITES

Asti *spumante* (sparkling)
Barsac
Eiswein
Gewürztraminer, Late-Harvest
Moscato
Muscat Beaume-de-Venise
Muscat Canelli
Muscat, Black
Muscat, Orange

Fruit, dessert, or just on their own

SWEET WHITES

Quarts de Chaume	Fruit, dessert, or just on their
Riesling, Late-Harvest	own
Riesling	
Spätlese	
Auslese	
Beerenauslese	
Trockenbeerenauslese	
(sweetest)	
Sauternes	
Tokay Aszu (puttonyos)	
Vin Santo	
Vouvray doux	

BLUSH AND ROSÉ WINES

DRY

Bandol Rosé	Most foods
Castel del Monte	
Chiaretto del Garda	
Côtes-de-Provence Rosé	
Sancerre Rosé	
Tavel	
Vin Gris	

OFF-DRY OR LIGHTLY SWEET

Cabernet d'Anjou	Cold meats, picnic fare
Grenache Rosé	
Rosé d'Anjou	
Rosé of Cabernet Sauvignon	
Rosé of Pinot Noir	
Vin Rosé	
White Zinfandel	
Zinfandel Rosé	

COMPATIBLE FOODS

LIGHT, FRUITY

Bardolino

Beaujolais

Bergerac

Blauburgunder

Bordeaux Supérieur

Bourgueil

Brouilly

Cabernet del Friuli

Cerasuolo

Chambourcin

Chinon

Chiroubles

Corbières

Côtes de Beaune-Villages

Côtes du Rhône

Côtes du Ventoux

Dolcetto D'Albia

Fitou

Foch

Freisa

Gamay

Gamay Beaujolais

Lambrusco

Italian Merlot

Napa Gamay

Saint-Amour

Sancerre Rouge

Saumur-Champigny

Valpolicella

All *nouveau*-style reds

Light meats, pizza, pasta, cheese dishes

RICH, CLASSIC, FULL-BODIED

Barbaresco

Beaune

Bordeaux (classified châteaux)

Cabernet Sauvignon

Chambolle-Musigny

Clos de Tart

Corton (*premier cru*)

Echézeaux

Fixin

Gevrey-Chambertin

La Romanée

Merlot

Morey-Saint-Denis

Nuits-Saint-Georges

Pernand-Vergelesses

Pommard

Sassicaia

Syrah

Taurasi

Tignanello

Vino Nobile di Montepulciano

Volnay

Vosne-Romanée

Roast lamb and beef, roast
goose, wild duck, cheese

ROBUST, VERY FULL-BODIED

Aglianico del Vulture

Amarone

Barolo

Brunello di Montalcino

Chambertin

Charbono

Châteauneuf-du-Pape

Clos Vougeot

Cornas

Venison, meat stews, strong
cheeses

ROBUST, VERY FULL-BODIED

Corton	Venison, meat stews, strong
Côte Rôtie	cheeses
Gigondas	
Hermitage	
La Tâche	
Mourvèdre	
Musigny	
Petite Sirah	
Richebourg	
Rhône varietal blends	
Romanée-Conti	
Sfursat	
Shiraz	
Syrah	
Zinfandel	

DESSERT REDS

Commanderia	Dried fruits, pound cake,
Madeira	fruitcake
Marsala	
Mavrodaphne	
Port	
Sherry	
Late-Harvest Zinfandel	

Wine and Food:
Winning Combinations

The suggested pairings of foods and wines below are intended only as a general guide. While many of them are proven matches, others reflect something of my own personal taste. Many other compatible relationships can be arranged, and you may make new discoveries of your own. All it takes is an adventurous spirit.

APPETIZERS AND FIRST COURSES

Antipasto	Dry white such as Pinot Grigio, Orvieto, Greco di Tufo; light red such as Chianti, Dolcetto, Valpolicella
Artichoke	*Stuffed*—Sauvignon Blanc, Pouilly-Fumé; *vinaigrette*—none
Asparagus	Fumé Blanc, Saint-Véran, dry Sylvaner
Avocado	*Stuffed with shellfish*—Johannisberg Riesling, Grey Riesling; *guacamole*—sangria
Brains	Beaujolais or other light red
Carpaccio	Dolcetto d'Alba, Barbera, Carmignano, Chianti Classico

Caviar	Champagne or other sparkling wine
Taramosalata	Sparkling Blanc de Noirs; or dry rosé
Céleri Rémoulade	White Graves, Sauvignon Blanc
Charcuterie (salami, sausages)	Beaujolais, Napa Gamay, Barbera, Dolcetto, Tocai, Vouvray, *vin gris*
Cold Meats (ham, roast beef, duck)	Light red or dry rosé, *vin gris*, Pinot Noir Blanc
Coquilles St. Jacques	Pouilly-Fumé, Fumé Blanc
Crudités	Fruity dry white like Mâcon Blanc, Italian Chardonnay, Pinot Bianco, dry Vouvray (*sec*); also Pinot Noir Blanc
Escargots	White Burgundy; Pouilly-Fumé
Foie Gras	Sauternes, Barsac, Alsace Gewürztraminer, Champagne rosé
Gravlax	Sauvignon Blanc, Gewürztraminer *vendange tardive;* also beer or aquavit
Pasta	*With shellfish*—Italian Chardonnay, Pinot Grigio, Gavi; *with cream sauce*—same; *with vegetables*—dry white, as above, or light red such as Cabernet del Friuli, Chianti, Beaujolais, Valtellina, Casal Thaulero, Corvo; *with meat*—light red, Barbera d'Alba, Rubesco, Rosso di Montalcino (see pasta chart on pages 103–05)
Pâtés, Liver	Vouvray, Alsace Gewürztraminer, Sancerre, Seyval Blanc; also light, fruity reds
Country Pâtés, Terrines	Medium-bodied red such as *cru* Beaujolais (Brouilly, Fleurie, Morgon), lighter red Bordeaux, Côtes du Rhône

Prosciutto and Melon	Dry fruity white such as Mâcon, Pinot Blanc, Pinot Grigio, Alsace Sylvaner, Grüner Veltliner, Vernaccia; also dry rosé, Pinot Noir Blanc
Quiche	Light red such as Côtes du Rhône, Chinon, Fleurie; also Alsace Riesling
Rillettes	Dry Vouvray, dry Chenin Blanc
Savory Canapés (salted nuts, cheeses)	Fino sherry, manzanilla, Champagne, dry Vermouth
Smoked Fish	
Smoked oysters or clams	Amontillado sherry; Tokay d'Alsace
Smoked salmon	Fino sherry, manzanilla, Champagne, California Sauvignon Blanc
Smoked trout	Lighter whites like Riesling *Kabinett*, Pinot Blanc, Sancerre
Soup	
Consommé, turtle, bisques	Fino or amontillado sherry; sercial or verdelho Madeira
French onion, lentil, pea	Beaujolais, Côtes du Rhône, Sauvignon, or Fumé Blanc
Other	Light, dry white; or none

FISH AND SHELLFISH

Abalone	Dry Riesling; dry, full-bodied rosé, such as Tavel; Grey or Early-Harvest Riesling; Pinot Gris
Bass, freshwater	Light dry white such as Soave, Pinot Bianco, unoaky Chardonnay

Bass, striped	*Grilled*—Saint-Véran; *baked or poached, with sauce*—full-bodied white Burgundy like Meursault or Puligny-Montrachet, California Chardonnay
Bluefish	Light reds like Volnay, Côte de Beaune-Villages, Auxey-Duresses rouge, Brouilly; also Sauvignon Blanc
Bouillabaisse	Côtes du Rhône Blanc, Tavel, Côtes-de-Provence red or dry rosé
Crab	*Cold*—Fumé Blanc or Pouilly-Fumé; *steamed or in sauce*—California Chardonnay
Crab, soft-shell	Dry, medium-bodied white like Sancerre, Saint-Véran, Sauvignon, or Fumé
Herring	Acidic white such as Muscadet, young Alsace Riesling
Lobster	California Chardonnay, Chablis *grand cru*, white Burgundy
Monkfish	Full-bodied California Chardonnay
Mussels	Muscadet, Gros Plant, Pinot Grigio
Oysters	French Chablis, Muscadet, Gros Plant, California Fumé Blanc
Quennelles	Chablis *grand cru*
Red Snapper	*Grilled*—Saint-Véran, Pouilly-Fuissé; *filets with sauce*—white Burgundy, Chardonnay
Salmon	*Cold, poached, with green sauce*—Sauvignon Blanc; *baked or grilled*—Hermitage Blanc, California Chardonnay; also medium reds such as nontannic Bordeaux, Beaune, Volnay, Beaune, Oregon Pinot Noir

Sardines	*Grilled*—crisp, dry white like Vinho Verde, Gros Plant, Muscadet; *smoked*—dry sherry
Scallops	Sauvignon Blanc, Puilly-Fumé, Sancerre, French Chablis, Gavi, Chardonnay
Shad, Shad Roe	Sauvignon Blanc, white Graves; also light Pomerol or Côtes du Rhône
Shark	Sancerre, Sauvignon Blanc, Saint-Véran
Shellfish	Generally, a crisp, tart white; see specific names
Shrimp	*Cocktail*—Muscadet, Pinot Blanc, dry Chenin Blanc; *scampi*—Chardonnay, Sauvignon Blanc, French Chablis; *Newburg*—Muscadet
Sole	Alsace Riesling, Riesling *Kabinett*, Pinot Bianco, Mâcon, light Chardonnay
Sashimi, Sushi	Sparking wines; light; dry or off-dry whites; sake; beer
Swordfish	*Grilled*—Sauvignon Blanc, also light red Burgundy; *with sauce and condiments*—full-bodied Chardonnay or Meursault
Trout	*Simple, grilled*—delicate white such as Mosel Riesling, dry Chenin Blanc, Lugana, Mâcon; *stuffed or with sauce*—fuller dry white; *smoked*—Riesling *Kabinett*, Pinot Blanc, Sancerre
Tuna	*White tuna salad*—light, fruity white such as Mâcon, dry Chenin Blanc, or dry rosé; *Salade nicoise*—Rhône white, Pinot Gris;

	grilled tuna steak—medium-bodied red like Merlot, Pomerol, Chinon (particularly for red-meat tuna); Santenay, Volnay
Turbot	Rich, full-bodied white Graves, white Burgundy, California Chardonnay

---

MEAT

Beef, Roast	Full-bodied reds: Cabernet Sauvignon, Merlot, Bordeaux, Barbaresco, mature Barolo, Vino Nobile di Montepulciano, Taurasi, Rioja Riserva
Beef Stew	Robust reds: Châteauneuf-du-Pape, Côte Rôtie, Gigondas, Spanna, Zinfandel, Dăo, Petite Sirah, Shiraz
Cassoulet (and meaty casseroles)	Cahors, Vacqueyras, Bergerac, Syrah, Barbera, Bandol; also lighter reds.
Chicken, Roast or Grilled	Medium-bodied red: Bordeaux, Cabernet, Merlot, Crozes-Hermitage, Côtes du Rhône, Gattinara; also full-bodied dry whites like Chardonnay
Chicken, Sautéed	*In cream sauce*—white Graves, white Burgundy, California Chardonnay; *Provençale*—Côtes du Rhône, Morgon; *coq au vin*—traditionally a red Burgundy (the same in which the dish is cooked), also Rhône reds

Chicken Salad	Riesling, dry Chenin Blanc, California Gewürztraminer, Vouvray
Confit d'oie	Firm red such as Médoc, Saint-Emilion; or full-flavored white like Alsace Gewürztraminer
Duck, Goose	Red Burgundy, California Pinot Noir; also Riesling *Spätlese,* Alsace Gewürztraminer *vendange tardive*
Frankfurters	Riesling, Beaujolais, beer
Game	Robust reds such as Chambertin, Clos Vougeot, Corton, Cornas, Côte Rôtie, Hermitage, Barolo, Brunello di Montalcino, Shiraz
Gamebirds	Lighter red Burgundy like Pommard, Volnay, Oregon Pinot Noir
Grilled Meats	Flavorful reds such as young Cabernet Sauvignon, Grumello, Inferno, Saint-Joseph, Crozes-Hermitage, Moulin-à-Vent, Barbera
Ham	Pinot Noir Blanc, *vin gris,* Tavel; also light reds like Beaujolais (chilled) or Chinon
Hamburger	Beaujolais-Villages, Saumur-Champigny, Napa Gamay, Zinfandel
Hare	Sturdy red, such as Gigondas, Côte Rôtie, Vino Nobile
Lamb, Roast	Mature Bordeaux, Cabernet Sauvignon or Merlot, Sassicaia, Rioja Riserva, Tignanello
Lamb Stew	Same as for roast lamb, but younger reds are suitable; also Australian Shiraz

Liver, Kidney, Sweetbreads	Fruity red such as Beaujolais, light Bordeaux, Côtes du Rhône or lighter Burgundy like Volnay, Pommard, or Beaune
Partridge, Pheasant	Red Burgundy like Volnay, Pommard, Monthélie, Fixin, Morey-Saint-Denis; California Pinot Noir or Syrah
Pork, Roast	*With fruit or herb stuffing*—Riesling *Kabinett* or *Spätlese;* if not too spicy, light reds like Fleurie, Morgon, Chénas
Rabbit	Medium-bodied red such as Merlot, Saint-Joseph, Chianti Classico, Moulin-à-Vent
Sausage	*Italian sausage dishes*—sturdy reds like Barbera, Chianti Riserva, Rubesco, Montepulciano; *saucisson chaud*—Beaujolais-Villages, Napa Gamay, Côtes du Rhône
Spareribs, Barbecued	Beaujolais, Zinfandel, Dolcetto
Steak	Firm, full-bodied red such as California Cabernet, Gigondas, Barbaresco, Chianti Riserva, Syrah, Shiraz, Saint-Emilion
Steak teriyaki	Zinfandel
Tripe	Firm, dry white like Crozes-Hermitage, Torgiano, Greco di Tufo; also Rosé d'Anjou
Turkey, Roast	*With trimmings*—Zinfandel or full-bodied Chardonnay, Merlot, Beaujolais *nouveau; salad*—light dry or off-dry white; *sandwiches*—same, but also light reds like cooled Beaujolais

Veal	*Chops, stew, scallops with mushrooms or marsala*—medium-bodied Bordeaux, Cabernet Sauvignon, Carmignano, Chianti Classico; *à la crème*—white Burgundy or Chardonnay; *milanese*—Gattinara
Venison	Lusty red such as Hermitage, Cornas, Barolo, Côte Rôtie, Amarone, Petite Sirah, Zinfandel; *grilled rare*—red Burgundy such as Chambolle-Musigny, Vosne-Romanee, Beaune

OTHER MAIN DISHES

Chili con Carne	Chilled Beaujolais or light Zinfandel; sangria, rosé, beer
Chinese Food	Crisp, spicy whites like Gewürztraminer, Tocai, Grüner Veltliner, Tokay d'Alsace; *richly sauced meats*—sturdy reds like Gigondas, Zinfandel, Petite Sirah; *hot, spicy dishes*—beer, dry or off-dry rosés, Gewürztraminer
Choucroute Garnie	Alsace Riesling; beer
Couscous	Cabernet Franc, Fleurie, Côtes du Rhône; also dry rosés like Tavel or Roditys
Curry	*Fish or chicken*—Riesling *Spätlese* (Rhinepfalz), Tokay d'Alsace; *lamb or beef*—chilled Beaujolais or young fruity Zinfandel
Eggplant	*Stuffed or parmigiana*—sturdy red such as Barbera d'Alba, Chianti, Bandol

Greek, Middle Eastern	See Mediterranean Section, pages 147–48
Japanese	Sake, light dry whites like Mâcon, lager beer
Meat Salads (smoked duck, chicken, turkey)	*Vin gris*, Beaujolais-Villages, Pinot Blanc, Pinot Noir
Mexican	Sangria, Rioja blanco, Beaujolais (chilled), beer
Moussaka	Côtes du Rhône, Vacqueyras, Roditys
Paella	Coronas, Rioja (red or white)
Pasta	See *Appetizers*
Pizza	Simple red like Chianti, Barbera, Dolcetto; also Beaujolais, light Zinfandel, Côtes du Rhône
Soufflé	*Cheese*—medium-bodied red Bordeaux, Rhônes, Pinot Noir; *fish*—delicate dry white like Mosel Riesling, Pinot Bianco, Soave Classico
Soup, Hearty (lentil, pea, onion, pot-au-feu)	Medium reds such as Côtes du Rhône, Cahors, Corbières, Chilean Cabernet
Thai Food	Light, crisp whites like Mâcon, Chenin Blanc, Pinot Bianco, Trebbiano, California Riesling, or Gewürztraminer; *spicy meats*—Beaujolais *nouveau*, beer
Vegetarian	Many light whites will work, depending on heaviness of dish. Rich bean dishes can take light reds; avoid tannic reds

Note: Sometimes the best way to set up a fine red wine, particularly an old one, is with nothing more than a mildly savory cheese such as Bel Paese, Cantal, Emmenthaler (Swiss), or a mild Brie. I find that the most versatile cheese for solid red wines (Cabernet, Merlot, Pinot Noir, Syrah, Sangiovese) is *chèvre* (goat cheese).

Asiago	Barbera d'Alba, Rubesco, Nebbiolo d'Alba; *aged Asiago*—bigger red like Barbaresco
Bel Paese	Gattinara, Valtellina reds, mature Bordeaux, or Cabernet Sauvignon
Blue, Creamy (Bleu de Bresse, Dolcelatte, Bavarian, Saga)	Fruity whites like Riesling; fruity, nontannic reds
Blue, Piquant (Blue Cheshire, Pipo Crem', Gorgonzola, Bleu d'Auvergne, Stilton)	Sturdy reds from Bordeaux or the Rhône, Vino Nobile, Rioja Riserva, Barbaresco
Blue, Pungent (Aged Gorgonzola, Roquefort, Danish Blue, Maytag Blue)	Sauternes, Barsac, Muscat Beaumes-de-Venise, Late-Harvest Zinfandel, Amarone, ruby port
Brie, Camembert	Merlot, Pomerol
Cheddar	*Mild Cheddar*—light reds; *well-aged Cheddar*—young Bordeaux, Rhône, Cabernet Sauvignon
Cheshire	Dry Mosel Riesling, Fleurie, Bourgogne rouge, Côtes du Rhône; also beer or cider
Cream Cheese (double or triple crème)	Full-bodied whites, medium-bodied reds, or Champagne
Edam	Medium-bodied reds

Époisses	Nuits-Saint-Georges, Chambolle-Musigny, Pommard, Corton-Bressandes
Fontina Val d'Aosta	Nebbiola d'Alba, Gattinara, Valtellina reds
Goat (*chèvre*)	Sancerre, Fumé Blanc, Saint-Véran; Cabernet Sauvignon, Syrah, Merlot; also Pinot Noir, Rhône reds and *cru* Beaujolais
Gouda	Fruity whites like Riesling; *aged Gouda*—sturdy reds, as for Cheddar
Gruyère, Emmenthaler	Medium-bodied dry whites, especially from the Rhône: Crozes-Hermitage Blanc, Condrieu; most reds
Monterey Jack	Light fruity reds like Napa Gamay, Gamay Beaujolais; also fruity whites like Chenin Blanc, Colombard, or Riesling. *Dry Jack*—firm Cabernet Sauvignon, Merlot, Zinfandel
Munster, Alsace	Alsace Gewürztraminer, robust reds
Parmigiano-Reggiano	Full-bodied Italian reds, such as Barbaresco, Barbera, Vino Nobile, Brunello di Montalcino, Ruffino Riserva Ducale, Badia a Coltibuono Riserva
Pecorino (and other sheep's milk cheeses)	Sturdy Italian reds, as above
Pont l'Évêque, Livarot	Sturdy reds, hard cider
Port Salut, Saint Nectaire, Pyrénées mountain cheese	Fruity whites like Vouvray, Riesling; also medium reds like Côtes du Rhône, Corbières, Cahors, light Bordeaux
Reblochon	Red Burgundy, California Pinot Noir, Hermitage, Châteauneauf-du-Pape

Ricotta Salata (young Pecorino)	Dry white such as Orvieto *secco*, Vernaccia di San Gimignano; also Sancerre, Fumé-Blanc
Roquefort	Sauternes or Barsac; also Late-Harvest Zinfandel
Semisoft Cheese	See *Port Salut*
Stilton	Vintage or ruby port
Telemes	Light, fruity California whites or reds
Tilsit	Grüner Veltliner, Tokay d'Alsace, dry Riesling; also medium-bodied to fairly sturdy reds
Tommes (semifirm mountain cheeses)	Medium-bodied Rhône reds, Zinfandel, Barbera
Vacherin Mont d'Or	Mature Pomerol or red Burgundy from the Côte de Beaune
Wensleydale	Dry, fruity whites, or light reds

DESSERTS

Note: A glass of fine sweet wine often makes an excellent dessert in itself, especially after a rich, multicourse meal and several wines preceding it. Very sweet, syrupy desserts will overwhelm dessert wines.

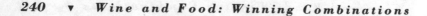

Apples	Too tart for most wines unless combined with cheeses like Appenzeller, Gruyère, Port Salut, Gouda, Monterey Jack; then only with light reds or whites. Pippins and Granny Smiths go with Port.
Baked Alaska (and other meringues)	Asti *spumante*, *crémant* Champagne
Berries (strawberries, raspberries, blackberries, blueberries)	Fresh strawberries and raspberries go with light fruity reds like Beaujolais or Zinfandel; also with lightly sweet Rieslings and Muscats
Cakes	German *Auslese, Beerenauslese,* sweet Muscats, Asti *spumante,* Extra Dry Champagne, Madeira
Cheesecake	Quarts de Chaume, sweet Vouvray
Creams, Custards, Puddings, Tarts	Sweet Vouvray, Sauternes
Fruit, Fresh	Off-dry whites like Riesling, Gewürztraminer, Chenin Blanc; *with cheese*—light reds and sweeter whites. Acid fruits like peaches, plums, citrus, and cherries fight wine unless cooked in cakes or custards, or in tarts
Fruitcake	Bual or malmsey Madeira, ruby or tawny port, dry oloroso sherry
Fruit Flambés (crêpes suzettes, cherries jubilee, bananas Foster)	Brandy
Fruit Tarts	Sauternes, Barsac, Riesling *Auslese*
Ice Cream	Too sweet for most wines, except perhaps Marsala; best with fruit liqueurs
Nuts	Tawny port, vintage port, Madeira

Pears	Late-Harvest Riesling, Riesling *Auslese;* excellent with creamy blue cheeses and Sauternes or Barsac
Plum Pudding	Ruby port, Late-Harvest Zinfandel
Sorbets	Like ice cream, better with fruit liqueurs such as cassis, blackberry, fraise des bois
Soufflés, Dessert	Sauternes, Late-Harvest Rieslings; Tokay Aszu
Strawberries	*Fresh*—lightly chilled red like Beaujolais or Zinfandel; *shortcake*—sweet Vouvray
Trifle	Medium-sweet sherry such as Bristol Milk
Zabaglione	Marsala

BIBLIOGRAPHY

Bugialli, Giuliano. *Classic Techniques of Italian Cooking*. New York: Simon and Schuster, 1982.

Child, Julia. *The French Chef Cookbook*. New York: Alfred A. Knopf, 1968.

———. *From Julia Child's Kitchen*. New York: Alfred A. Knopf, 1970, 1981.

———. *The Way to Cook*. New York: Alfred A. Knopf, 1989.

Claiborne, Craig. *The New York Times Cookbook*, revised edition. New York: Harper & Row, 1990.

Clark, Ann. *Ann Clark's Fabulous Fish*. New York: New American Library, 1987.

David, Elizabeth. *French Provincial Cooking*. New York: Harper & Row, 1962.

——— *French Country Cooking*. London: Penguin, 1962.

Fisher, M. F. K. *The Art of Eating*. New York: The World Publishing Company, 1954.

———. *With Bold Knife and Fork*. New York: Paragon Books, 1969.

Goldstein, Joyce. *The Mediterranean Kitchen*. New York: William Morrow, 1989.

Hazan, Marcella. *The Classic Italian Cookbook*. New York: Alfred A. Knopf, 1973.

Hom, Ken. *East Meets West*. New York: Fireside Books, 1987.

Jaffrey, Madhur. *Madhur Jaffrey's Cookbook*. New York: Harper and Row, 1989.

Kafka, Barbara. *Microwave Gourmet*. New York: William Morrow, 1987.

Lewis, Edna. *A Taste of Country Cooking*. New York: Alfred A. Knopf, 1989.

Madison, Deborah. *Greens*. New York: Bantam Books, 1987.

Memphis Cook Book, The. Memphis: The Junior League of Memphis, Inc. 1952.

Rosso, Julie, and Sheila Lukins. *The Silver Palate Cookbook*. New York: Workman Publishing 1982.

———. *The New Basics*. Workman Publishing, 1989.

Smith, Jeff. *The Frugal Gourmet Cooks with Wine*. New York: William Morrow, 1986.

Torres, Marimar. *The Spanish Table*. New York: Doubleday, 1986.

Tropp, Barbara. *The Modern Art of Chinese Cooking*. New York: William Morrow, 1982.

Waters, Alice. *Chez Panisse: Pasta, Pizza and Calzone*. New York: Random House, 1984.

Wells, Patricia. *Bistro Cooking*. New York: Workman Publishing, 1989.

Wolfert, Paula. *The Cooking of Southwest France*. New York: Dial Press, 1983.

I N D E X

Chardonnay, 23, 25, 34, 41, 66, 107, 108, 114, 130, 231, 233
Chenin Blanc, 29, 130
Fumé Blanc, 127–28, 231
Gewurztraminer, 26, 127, 234
Merlot, 65–66, 145, 204
Pinot Blanc, 104, 130
Pinot Noir, 65, 89, 90, 114, 234, 235, 239
Rhône varietals or blends, 26, 88, 91–92, 98, 148, 204
Riesling, 101–2, 104, 114, 126, 237
Sauvignon Blanc, 93, 111, 230
sparkling, 39, 86–87, 147
Syrah, 98, 148, 204
vin gris, 131, 145
see also Zinfandel
Calvados, 35, 175, 182, 184, 185
Cambodian cuisine, 125
Camembert, 45, 184, 238
Campari, 41
Canapés, 27, 34, 180, 230
Cantal, 44, 238
Capezzana (Tuscany), 60–61
Capon, 111, 119
Cardinal, 160
Caribbean Sunset, 161–62
Carmenet, 29, 43, 129, 204
Carmignano, 91, 98, 105, 111, 228, 236
Carneros, Domaine, 86
Carpaccio, 228
Cassis, 39–40, 148, 158
Cassoulet, 93, 98, 233
Castel del Monte, 60, 203, 224
Caviar, 27, 34, 81, 229
Cavit, 88, 155
Caymus, 43, 67
Céléri rémoulade, 229
Cellaring wine, 36, 187, 200–205
Cerasuolo, 225
Ceretto, Bruno, 186
Chablis, 24, 92, 93, 98, 130, 223
French, 92, 104, 109, 137, 203, 223, 231, 232
Chalone, 130, 131
Chambertin, 88, 89, 226, 234
Chambolle-Musigny, 226, 236, 239
Chambourcin, 225
Champagne, 27, 34, 38–40, 46, 59, 60, 81, 82–86, 87, 93, 98, 114, 132, 143, 145, 158, 192, 204, 210, 211, 215, 229, 230, 238, 241
cocktail, 40, 88, 161
making of, 83–84, 86, 88

opening, 198–99
punches, 88, 124, 163, 164, 166
three levels of, 84–86
use of term, 82–83
Chandon, Domaine, 39, 132
Chapelle-Chambertin, 65
Charbaut, 85
Charbono, 226
Charcuterie, 229
Chardonnay, 42, 67, 78, 84, 87, 93, 98, 101–2, 104, 105, 106, 107, 111, 119, 128–31, 133, 143, 144, 149, 154, 190–91, 203, 221, 223, 230, 232, 233, 235, 236
California, 23, 25, 34, 41, 66, 107, 108, 114, 130, 231, 233
Italian, 25, 102, 104, 105, 131, 146, 203, 229
Chassagne-Montrachet, 105, 119, 204, 223
Châteauneuf-du-Pape, 88, 91, 98, 145, 146, 148, 204, 226, 233, 239
Cheddar, 26, 44, 45, 91, 111, 176, 238
Cheesecake, 241
Cheeses, cheese courses, 26, 35, 38, 41, 42, 44–45, 91, 110–11, 125, 133, 176, 177, 184, 221–22, 223, 225, 226–27, 238–40. See also specific cheeses
Chénas, 132, 203, 235
Chenin Blanc, 26, 28, 29, 87, 101–2, 104, 107–8, 118, 130, 144, 203, 223, 230, 232, 234, 237, 239, 241
Cheshire, 238
Chèvre. See Goat cheese
Chianti, 27, 64, 78, 98, 103, 105, 114, 147, 148, 203, 204, 228, 229, 235, 236, 237
Chiaretto del Garda, 25, 60, 203, 224
Chicken, 42, 65–66, 77, 78, 98, 102, 111, 125, 130, 137, 143, 144, 145, 146, 148, 149, 221–22, 223, 233–34
Chilean wines, 104, 237
Chili con carne, 236
Chilling wine, 27, 193–94
Chinese cuisine, 24–25, 77, 125, 127, 142, 143–44, 236
Chinon, 62, 98, 119, 225, 230, 233, 234
Chiroubles, 63, 132, 203, 225
Chocolate, 27, 28
Choucroute garnie, 61, 77, 125, 236
Christmas, 81, 82, 89, 93, 97
Christmas Punch, 165–66
Cider, 238, 239
Cinsaut, 91, 148

Grapes, harvesting of, 55–56
Grappa, 186
Gratien & Meyer, 87
Graves, 23, 34, 43, 108, 113, 203, 204, 222, 229, 232, 233
Gravlax, 229
Gray, Penelope, 139
Greco di Tufo, 105, 146, 223, 228, 235
Greek cuisine, 129
Greek wines, 148, 149
Grenache, 91, 148, 203, 224
Grgich Hills, 107, 130
Grignolino, 25, 137
Gros Plant, 109, 231, 232
Grumello, 57, 103, 105, 132, 234
Grüner Veltliner, 221, 230, 236, 240
Gruyère, 239

Hacienda, 29, 104
Hagafen Cellars, 114
Ham, 113, 118, 137, 234
Hamburger, 234
Hare, 90, 234
Harvest dinners, 56–59, 70
Harvests, 55–56
Harvey's Sherry, 180
Heidsieck, Charles, 85
Heidsieck Monopole, 85
Heitz Cellars, 36
Hennessy, 182, 183
Henriot, 85
Hermitage, 55, 88, 90–91, 98, 204, 223, 227, 231, 234, 236, 239
Herring, 231
Hine, 183
Hock glassware, 192
Hogue, 66, 104, 126
Hugel, 127
Humidity, for cellaring, 201–2

Ice cream, 180, 241
Idaho wines, 67
Indian cuisine, 77, 125, 129, 137, 145–146
Indonesian cuisine, 125
Inferno, 57, 132, 234
Inglenook, 128, 129
Iron Horse Vineyards, 39, 58–59, 86, 113, 129, 130
Israeli wines, 114
Italian cuisine, 64, 147–48. *See also* Pasta
Italian wines:
  Chardonnay, 25, 102, 104, 105, 131, 146, 203, 229

Merlot, 203, 225
  rosés, 60–61, 148
  see also specific wines and vineyards

Jaboulet, 155
Jade Mountain, 91
Jaeger, Lila, 65
Japanese cuisine, 146–47, 237
Jekel, 126
Jermann, 98, 119, 186
Jordan, 43, 86
Jota, La, 91, 92
Juliénas, 62, 63, 77, 132, 203
Junot, Rene, 154, 155

Kabinett, 25, 40, 42, 118, 119, 125, 142, 145, 146, 204, 230, 232, 235
Kamman, Madeleine, 58
Keehn, Karen, 58
Kendall-Jackson, 67, 128, 132
Kenwood, 129, 132
Kid, 149
Kidney, 235
Kir (*Vin Blanc Cassis*), 158, 159–60
Kir Royal, 39–40, 158, 160
Kirsch, 175, 182, 185
Klug, 127
Korbel, 86
Kornell, Hanns, 86
Kosher wines, 113–14
Krug (France), 84, 85, 86
Krug, Charles (Calif.), 36

Lachryma Christi Rosso, 105
Lafite, Château, 195
Lamb, 24, 25, 42, 55, 56–57, 66, 76, 77, 111, 119, 146, 148, 149, 226, 234
Lambrusco, 64, 137, 225
Larose-Trintaudon, 204
Latour, Château, 195, 214
Laurent-Perrier, 85
Lembey, 88, 132
Lemon, 27–28
Lichine, Alexis, 31
Light, 202
Lillet, 38, 41
Liqueurs, 175, 241, 242
Lirac, 147, 148, 203
Livarot, 111, 184, 239
Liver, 229, 235
Lobster, 104, 130, 144, 231
Lohr, J., 64